How the Earth
Holds Us

How the Earth Holds Us

POEMS

Mary Holman Tuteur

Copyright © 2023 by John Tuteur Trustee,
Maggie Tuteur Revocable Trust
All rights reserved

ISBN: 978-1-941066-60-7
Library of Congress Control Number: 2023905484

Art:
Mary Holman Tuteur

Cover and interior photos:
Louise Kleinsorge Williams

Design:
Jo-Anne Rosen

Wordrunner Press
Petaluma, California
www.wordrunner.com

Printed in the United States of America

To all the humans, animals,

landscapes, and spirits

that are the source of my inspiration

Contents

BUCKEYES

THE SHYEST, LONGEST LOVE

THIS POEM IS NOW THE MAKER

Foreword

The things we need to give meaning to our lives, as I see it, never come purely from inside or outside of ourselves—they come from the mix. Maggie Tuteur was lucky enough to have a special connection with her friend Lulu Williams's family, who gave Maggie a copy of Robert Louis Stevenson's *A Child's Garden of Verses* when she was eight. This book offered Maggie a doorway to self-expression and creativity for the next sixty or so years of her life.

Maggie's enchantment with poetry and her use of it enriched her and those who have read and appreciated her work. *Enchantment* is a good word for Maggie's relationship with poetry. She entered a kind of reverie when she read and wrote poetry. It was her language. Her use of it for healing and moving forward in her life is worthy of our attention. The act of writing poetry offered her strength and solace in dealing with her internal struggles and the pain of her mother's and her best friend's deaths.

How Maggie dealt with the academic side of her poetry pursuit was remarkable. She went to Stanford Graduate School in English Literature with no other ambition than to write. She was awarded her master's degree because of that love, not for her academic prowess.

As I write this, my memory summons an image of Maggie and me sitting in a café in Petaluma, where she was sharing a poem she had just written about her mother ("In Another Country"). Her enthusiasm and verve are what strike me now. When I look back at such times—when she had just finished a poem or just come back from a poetry class—I remember how present she was in those sharings. There was an intensity that she brought when sharing that part of herself that I remember now.

It is my hope that this book of Maggie's poetry will be a cherished gift not just to those of us who knew her but also to those who never met her, and that in these pages her spirit and her love of words will live on.

—Bruce Gibbs
    September 2022

NEGATIVE SPACE

A Long Life

How precious is our death
as we imagine it, now and again:
the death at the white rapids in the river,
or ending the dive from the high rocks into the river;
the rattlesnake sliding through camp at night;
the warm eyes of the doctor who confesses your disease.
Your first lover is eighteen, driving too fast.
As the car leaves the road,
you see only each other's eyes.

But this is not your own death;
that one hums beneath your breath
too familiar to hear.
This is your dream-death, your darling confessor
who tunes your life like a piano,
who irradiates your hours with his attention,
who intrigues you with your own final gestures
so that you imagine them, over and over,
throughout a long life.

The Second Day

He isn't what you would call   alive   today
but still   he streaks by me,
white flash in the corner of my eye
as I rustle in my reading chair   book unopened,
cold coffee in my hands.
Or through me in the garden   cornering fast
'round sprawling lilacs   giddy with bees.

I spin around   incredulous: he's not wearing
his flesh   his bones   his well-fondled fur.
Comforted each time his shining body circles back,
scoping out his earthly home   from bold new perspectives.

I stay within the boundaries   of our common life,
Watering   pacing   moving beneath thought,
cultivating a still place   so both of us
know where I am.

Grace for My Twenty-Fifth Year

These years, with their open grasses,
have been good to me, have wintered me
and brought me up through spring.
The oak trees are continuous
in reaching into sun.
The golden bowls of harvesting I bring.

I am living in the echo
of a clear bell's ring.

Coming Up

The great, sonorous turning has begun, my friend, but you don't
    know it.
The tides are deep, even in your own familiar body,
and the origins of movement
are a secret you keep from yourself.
You who can feel
the whale pass beneath you in the depths
through the curious calming of the waves about your kayak
cannot feel this turning.
When Neptune unforks your fishy tail,
you turn and turn in his cave at the bottom of the sea,
you furl and unfurl to recover the shimmer of motion.
You re-create each step life takes, coming into its own.
You let yourself
know slowly that you are rising, trilling,
that you are a body stretching up
through watery light,
that you will break the surface
with a great, gaping breath
bursting forth one more time among the living.

Invocation

My mother, bedazzled
by her image in the water,
ate the moon the same way
she used to swallow oysters,
head thrown back to elongate
the slick passage down.

The moon, beguiled
by my mother's serpentine appetite,
went on down as eager as a child on a slide.
She lives at that chilled center now,
a fading opal, floating on her back.

My mother, stunned
by the emptiness invading her water mirror,
has wasted away and petrified, her body
a boat nosed by aimless currents.
The moon mistakes her own memories
of indigo reflections for vain imaginings.

Bestir yourselves, dark waters,
from dreams of your own darkness,
and bear down. Out of the splintering
boat of my dead mother,
birth the moon.

Sitting Still

In memory of Scott Glasscock

The tide was receding, the three of us sitting
on a strand of shining sand, mirroring
the sunset back into itself—land and sky
permeated by each other.
We were caught in the translucence,
transfixed between the elements
by an almost lurid hue. Gelatinous. Blood orange.
Laughable, really. Except that we were engulfed.

We had come here with your lover, Don,
who was wasting of the slow plague,
and none of us knew how to sit with that.
We had come to the ocean for help, but what we got
was a further strangeness, stripping away
our capacity for giddiness or terror.
We'd been taken out beyond, but without leaving.
When we returned, we were almost ashamed.

We never talked about it. Don died
without knowing what to say about death.
I held his feet as his body gave up its warmth.
And then you, my spirit buddy, keeper of my secrets,
on the riptide of a brutal, unexpected illness,
without asking me if you could go.

Sometimes I think I am alone here but
for that moment which lit us in its harsh, absurd beauty.
Because it took us in, like an afterimage,
we shimmer there.

These Days

These days, roses, wisteria assault us
with the stubborn persistence of life.
Peonies, unfurling, expand my breath
as pollen forces tears straight down my face.

Pollen, and the restless knowledge
that in his city, sixteen hours up the coast,
my friend lies down along the lip of death's wide cup,
makes himself comfortable. April sun,
a clean breeze bearing the scent of jasmine
through an open window.

He was a gardener once, but these days
he feels no need to see the rooted plants.
His body knows them as well as it knows
the peaches he pickled all summer as a boy.
He isn't looking backward into stories of who he's been,
or forward into that stunning moment
when his cells release their molecules back to stardust.
He's looking upward into light
rebounding off the ceiling.

His lover, Jimi, brings him pain pills, lattes, the daily *Times*.
They chatter, or they're silent, or sometimes they cry
into each other's arms.

After Your Stroke

For Jericho

You were balancing, when I met you, on the cusp of old age,
but you took me back with you to the nights
of the Russian River's open-air dance hall
when Old Blue Eyes was just learning his phrasing.
Let me watch you take a swig from your hip flask
while he crooned to the girls in their angora sweaters,
and you'd slick back your pompadour and move in on one
who stood trembling on the blond wood floor between numbers,
her palms sweaty and malleable in the sandy night.

You'd swing me like you used to swing her
out across the floor and wind me
back into your torso with one seamless gesture.
I felt so safe, swimming in the nonchalance of your gaze.
You escorted me through the world as it was
before I was born into it.

Now you grapple with my simple name.
I pour myself into your gaze
the way I did when we were dancing.
If I give you the rhythm, I figure,
the next step will come up through your feet.
But your mind skids out from under you.
And love be damned, I watch you skitter back across
the dull sheen of ice unfolding between us.

No detail holds its place in the spreading void.
Not the punch line to a joke, not the bar from a stray jazz riff.
You recede into the iris of your own eye,
and I feel it, right beneath your ribcage,
that instant when you let me go mid-swing
and I spin out, a lonely note
to some old love song you won't hum again.

New Year's, 2007

I went out on impulse, early,
to prune the roses this morning.
A skill my father taught me, brutal
and discreet. He's gone now,
and all his orderly beds
that put my tumult of over-reaching branches,
my thick stalks of deadwood, to shame.

That would have been his word, *shame.*
He feared, tried to tolerate my chaos,
how I came at first from all directions.
For him there was always a time and a place.
But if I could ask his help right now, he'd
throw his long shears over his shoulder
and step out to meet me on the first,
to remind me of the "right" way.
We did our best together out-of-doors,
he and I, surrounded by enough space
for his strict and my wild to coexist.

Why am I talking about my father again?
I meant to talk about resolutions, how I
ignore the restrictions I impose on myself.
Half of my resolutions, and it's only January 10th.
I'd rather talk about pruning, how my father showed me
to cut each branch at a slant, just a pink nodule,
to keep the nascent growth from rotting.
But before that we hacked away all the good growth,
branch after curving branch, and all the upstart canes,
cutting through to the heart of the matter.
Here we lean together, with all our tools and tendencies,

to commune with the stark and leafless.
Each cut is crucial now, asking discipline as well as intuition
to reveal to the plant and to ourselves
the spare and unpredicted shape
of its initial thrust.

Negative Space

In memory of my birth mother

All I've felt is her absence,
though I know her heartbeat in my cells.
That must be true. That first pulsing
as cell upon cell divides itself from itself against
a background of rhythm that wraps us.
And the sounds of her birth-cries must live on in some
layer of my memory, but not, I imagine,
the sound of the hospital door closing behind her, just
the appalling silence that belled out in her wake.

As I grew, I ran my fingers over my own face, self-born, feeling
for the pulse of my own heart. Learning
the diurnal rhythms, the rhythms of family,
of skipping and reading, city and pasture.
She was the void just over my shoulder.
She was not-knowing.

I grew up to track her down, picking up haphazard clues,
slipping between the sealed-record laws, and I wrote to her.
Asking for one meeting. Face to face. She answered: *No.*
Behind her tidy life, her job, two sons and her husband,
I was the gap in her universe.
She wasn't going to turn around.

By the time her sons, selling their childhood home,
went through her papers and found my letter,
it was eighteen years later, and she
was a widowed, wordless Alzheimer's patient
trapped in a nursing home with others who,

abandoned in the halls in wheelchairs,
cried *Help!* out loud all day
and never knew who came.

But everyone who saw me knew me as her daughter.
I walked in and faced my own face gaping, recognizing me.
I sat at her bedside and we pressed palms, our hands
finding the rhythm to a dance that skimmed the bedclothes.
As we were in the beginning, beyond words.

Today, over her coffin, I stare down into her face
that had been our face. Run a hand over both our brows,
finger the trail down to the corners of each mouth.

I almost faint, as up from her casket
a harsh breath reaches out to pull me down.
Blood brothers and cousins break my fall.
I feel the gap in the universe closing over.
I hear the silence behind the silence
where the echo of her absence does not ring.

Birds Bearing South

The sky is black with small birds bearing south.
A swarm of heartbeats bears into the wind.
A swath of fabric spins itself anew
with every breath. But are they breathing now?
Or does the wind they fly into expand their lungs?
I want to know if they are of one mind,
grave pleasure swelling them, en masse, or does
each member stir up its own joy and thrill
to feel a multitude respond in kind?
A joining of the "I and Thou" that we
might envy its complex simplicity.
And do they wonder, sensing us below,
if we know something they might want to know?

Aging

Once you know death's got you in his sights
some things rest easier:
That Daddy loved you best of all.
Or not.

That you and Francie opened
the same pale blue snow coats on Christmas
and strutted, arm in arm, around the neighborhood.
Or not.

That they picked you last for kickball,
that he brought you red ribbons,
that God listened to you in the kitchen garden.
Or not.

That you could seduce your mother
out of her windy spasms of grief
by making her laugh.
You could try. She could not.

And later, that plane geometry
was God's first language,
that your date was a good kisser,
that Mom finally swallowed all her pills
just like she threatened to,
that your stepmother bred bulldogs
and looked too much like you.
Or not. Or not.

There they are, a scatter of happenings back there
that meant the world to you,
that you thought might justify your life to you
or break you for good.

When you first sense death approaching you
from all directions, branch by branch,
then you know those times are over,
either way.

You feel this self here now, whose hard-won memories
have crackled and altered over time.
Did your lover really love you?
At the very instant you loved him?
Or a nanosecond later, when you'd given up
and were turning away?

Your regrets are those of someone you imagine.
And your pride. And your shame.
Your love for your ongoing saga.
Some other self will be there for the ending.
It's a relief once you let it sink in.

All you have is the present you breathe in.
Now…and now…and now the cat
pads into the study and summons you to bed.

At a Loss

I wasn't home the night my mother swallowed down her sleeping pills. I was cramming for exams with my high school dorm mates, fretting over college applications, boning up on the surfer stomp. We were setting each other's hair with fat pink rollers. Sucking on bobby pins. Humming Beach Boys songs: *Wish they all could be California girls.* We were California girls.

I wasn't home the next morning when they found her cooling in her bed. I was painting a streak of lavender eye liner over yellow eye shadow. Dreading first-period algebra class. Hoping to run into that boy in the hall. Giddy with beginnings. Leaving home.

Once they carried my mother down the front steps, there was no home to leave. The wrong boy stopped me in the hall and escorted me to the principal's office where the principal offered me a chair and broke the news when I was no longer standing but not yet sitting.

I didn't say a word. Not to the principal. Not to my father. Not to myself.

I impersonated myself. Flew east for college. Sang soprano in choir for the Bach B Minor Mass. Got down the atlas to find Vietnam.

I smiled politely as my father's new girlfriend, on her second martini, placed her finger on my eye tooth and wondered out loud, "Doesn't this look just like a fang?"

That wasn't me there, hitting the high notes. Swallowing insults. I was out of earshot. Stranded between the cocoon of girlhood and dawning hopes of womanhood. Hanging out in the ether. A stump of myself. I never left home. Home was dissolving around me while I leafed through *Seventeen* magazine, spouted Walt Whitman. A song of myself. Gazed into the mirror with my mouth full of bobby pins, sucking in their metal aftertaste.

Glimmerings

My mother didn't die like that, head thrown back and body
draped across the chaise longue, the way she drew it out for me.
The cord of her telephone wound and wound again
around her flaccid throat. That was a stage play,
her first big role: She strangled herself
when her man hung up on her.

She learned to smoke for that part, but smoking
didn't kill her either. No hacking,
spitting death. Though sometimes
I might have wished it on her as I sat
and listened to her lips suck languidly
on the plastic tip of her cigarette holder.
The blue-gray smoke coiled off her
as she leaned into her pale green chair
and assured me, again and again:
"It's impossible to strangle yourself—your hands
go slack as soon as you pass out."

Sometimes her sucking soothed me,
as habitual as the rhythmic gulping
of the golden carp circling our garden pond
that you could count on to shimmy its tail,
glimmer when the light was right, and gulp again.

My mother toyed with me and with herself
every time she repeated what couldn't happen
as the carp grew up to dwarf the pond,
and I shifted shape from the worshipful
daughter at her knee to the gangly brooder
hunched down across from her, feigning indifference.

Loathing the sounds and habits of her. Longing
for her to outlive my hatred.

She died in her own bed, no stage prop,
her long neck nestled deep into her pillow.
After the last swallow from her bathroom cup,
the last tablet from the vial with her name on its label.

There was no mistaking her, my mother,
who had passed the point where her own grasp relaxed,
her exhale rippled out in circles that still keep widening.
The breath that never breathes itself back in.
The carp that rises to the surface,
moonlight glinting off its scales.

The Grain in the Wood

His steadfast gait sets him off from the surge of tourists.
Passing on the street, you'd imagine him
wise and at ease in the world. Fissures and gullies
crease his face from crow's feet to jowl.

Facing dusk alone, he veers off
through the doors of the maritime museum,
settles in its small theater. They're screening
a documentary on the old ore carriers
that crisscrossed the Great Lakes
in the heyday of the big steel mills.

What he wants is darkness and a moment to place himself.
Visiting hours over, he's come from the bedside of his wife.
Younger than he, she'd been hardy, their private life raucous and
    reliable,
until she'd woken him at dawn in their island cabin
with harsh, spasmodic breathing. The local
doctor gave her days.

The lights go down and grainy old images
present themselves. He breathes. He watches.
Empties himself of everything personal,
fills himself with pictures of that boat up there.
Looking closely, he can see the grain in the wood.

The muscles in his palm tighten on the armrest.
Something palpable tugs at him from back beyond
the decaying ground of his marriage.
The deck and the railing of this precise boat.
Solid and specific. Known to his touch.

He'd been a boy back in Cleveland.
One time, his friend's father, the mill owner, gave them all
a birthday ride on a carrier across Lake Erie.
He had run his hands and eyes
along every surface he could see or touch.
So his body knew this boat. The curve of its railing,
the rounded, shallow ridges of its grain.

Not wisdom, not assurance holds him now
but a boy's love for the look of a curve and the feel of a grain.
Memory. Precision. The right film at the right time.
He finds himself, as actual
as polished wood, riding choppy water.

Airport

He might have been an angel at play
in the belly of the crunched metal dragonfly.
He bounced and tumbled, fringed with bright gold wings.
It was his to stream through glass, fly away home.
He was tiny and electric, that's what I saw at first,
looking down three stories from the guardrail of the garage.

He bounced and tumbled. He was tiny and electric.
I kept looking into what was happening.
A man on fire. Trapped in the cockpit.
Slamming his body against glass.

That was something nobody wanted to see.
People backed off as if blown by a physical force
while I clung to the guardrail. I didn't want
this man to be alone. He needed a witness,
or I needed to witness.

Hard to put it down even now, years later,
how he flung himself against glass and flame
and how he was flung.
Nervous system fending off, melting into
the anguish. Full partner
in the dance of fire.

Time Is a Road

Time is a road with a mind of its own.
It never promised to go straight.
Meanders through the cloud-ripe afternoon, let's say,
then back-tracks to recover your lover's younger face.
The face is chaste but hungry.
You are caught up again
in sharp, fresh desire.

Time is lonely. He paces
with the eons curled up in his back pocket.

He can crawl with the earthworm,
he can shimmy with light,
but he must move on.

Except, sometimes, when he senses,
in a temporal creature's naked love, an irrefutable need,
and we tangle, we open our fates to him.
We match his every rhythm, and time stops.

Time is in love with space.
She can undo him and wind him back again
with one deep sigh.

So he likes our company.
We go faster than light.
We can bring back the dead.

Solitude

Oh, solitude, you are not as solemn
as you would have us think, as fraught
with loneliness, boredom, spiritual angst.

Late last evening in my small city, a shy man,
a man who chafed for years behind
his bassoon in the symphony orchestra,
stomped across his bare floor
to the exacting beat of synthesized Bach.
Thrusting and parrying, he veered down the hall,
hands free and jubilant, to conduct
his own reddening face in the bathroom mirror.

Not as weighty, solitude,
as the sound of you leads us to believe.
Nearing midnight, in the playroom, the therapist
has dusted and straightened the motley toys
the children have infused with their private woes.
She makes small talk, dolls propped up around her,
pours them imaginary tea.

This morning in the suburbs, a housewife, deep-cleaning,
stumbles on old record albums, locks the doors,
pulls the curtains and lets her sore body down
onto the rug behind the couch.
where her hips unbuckle and her voice, long out of key,
rises to meet Janis Joplin's rude growl:
"Take another little piece of my heart now, baby . . ."

It's 3 A.M. The blocked novelist
abandons his obsessing to rearrange
the cacti clustered on his windowsill
so that they catch the moonlight along their spines.

Angels

The waves reach up and fall onto each other,
onto the beach with the same rhythm I heard in my childhood
as I dipped into sleep in my house above the beach.
Today, a day of stillness and full, gentle sun,
they rise up an opal-green, penetrated by the light.

The angels rise up, not out of, but of them,
a medium half fog, half cloud, half spirit.
Their outlines round like clouds, their shapes vague and all touching,
basking out of the ocean floor toward me.
Maybe they walk toward other things, everything,
but also toward me, specifically me.
Their long-ago listening, their thick legs striding together.
They are separate but identical, and one mass.
They move as a mass toward me.
They rise up through and off of the waves.

SOIL AND SEED

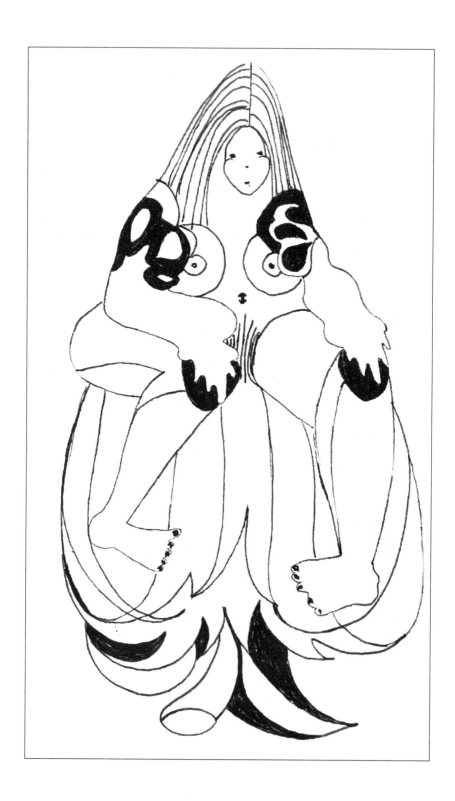

Shades of Childhood

Still daylight when they tucked me in. I could feel the flowers beneath my window flexing their petals for the fat yellow bees, sweet-natured bumblers that brushed my palms. June bugs, those ornery earth movers, lurching and bumbling. Upturned earthworms sensing the air with delicate snouts.

That was my place down there, not this holding pen of floppy dolls.

Just before firefly time, the shadows cast by venetian blinds began their twilight crawl across the ceiling, transporting me, breath by breath, into that night garden I could never anticipate, where I was the soil and the seed.

Source

My mother showed me.
She pulled a carrot
right up out of the ground
before my eyes.
She ran it under
the garden tap
and held it out to me,
still warm from the soil.

My baby teeth tested
its crisp, giving body.

In that one gesture
she secured me to the earth,
my mother on her knees in Ohio.

The Needle's Eye

You couldn't get meat in France right after the war,
except maybe horse. The belated corpses of cattle
melted into the fields. Even so, back home in Cleveland,
my family, American Jews around our Christmas tree,
mapped out our summer vacation to Europe.
Then the maid smoothing tissue paper to pack
father's tuxedo, mother's loganberry suit,
my organdy bathrobe. My dad let me
stack a whole suitcase full of American cigarettes
for him to dole out, pack by pack, to the bellboys and waiters,
a carton for each concierge who got us concert seats.
Fitting them in tight was like playing blocks
slippery with cellophane.

But what I remember most about the trip itself
is the staircase to the Ritz. It spread
across my whole horizon, pulling my eyes upward as it rose.
Motes of crystal embedded in granite
shot off shards of light as the sun struck them.
I felt daunted, as if that stern, long-bearded
God-of-our-fathers had clapped eyes on me.
Maybe *these* were the stairs to heaven!

But my father seemed dapper and at ease
as he tipped the cabbie, instructed the doorman
who wore a taupe uniform and white cotton gloves,
opened the car door for my mother,
and rolled oily sounds, new to my ear, around his tongue:
"Bonjour, monsieur, mesdames."
The same concierge from before the war
strode down the stairs to welcome *my* father by name.

I don't remember the reunion itself,
but my father recalled it to me over the years.
He believed the concierge took pleasure
in greeting his returning face,
and I did too, each time he repeated the story.
It took on for us the stature of a fairytale. My father's voice,
infused with an always-dawning confidence,
caressing it as though it were a talisman
he returned with tobacco-stained fingers.

He needed to believe that the courtesy,
deep courtesy or its veneer, could save him.
Could cull him, in his double-breasted suit and felt fedora,
from his brethren, their eyes appearing
huge in their sunken faces, who, even then,
as the doorman curled his glove around the taxi's gleaming handle,
crisscrossed Europe without ceremony, speaking the names
of loved ones they still might find among the living.

He needed to believe, and so did I, remembering the squeak
from my patent-leather Mary Janes as I pumped my way
up that vast and elegant staircase. Too young
to grasp the story behind the story. Strangely aware
of the long fall rolling out behind me.

Knowing What We Know

For Julius

A cowboy's tan runs upward from the base
of his Adam's apple and down
over stocky wrists and across ropey knuckles
out canny fingers that brush
fat horseflies off the pinto's haunches,
trim ragged hoofs, tighten girths, coil rope.

The skin beneath his shirt is as pale
as the moon's averted face,
shy of the sun and wind and sky
and of himself, I used to think as I watched him
roll up his sleeves and slide his forearm
into the water trough to skim off frogspawn or plunge it
deep into the round of a shorthorn's womb, dislodging
the calf jammed up in the birth canal.

A slow-talking man, a little abashed
about knowing what his hands knew,
about what tugs and what gives.
The first time a barn-spoiled pony took off with me,
I dropped the reins and hunkered down over his withers
as if wrestling control was something
I couldn't let myself know I could do.
I heard him whoop and kick his horse,
his hoofbeats gaining ground on me,
felt him pull my mare up short 'til I
uncoiled in the blessed standstill.
His fingers wove the reins back into mine.

"Now, push your heels down into your stirrups.
sit up tall in your saddle, but leave some give
in your hips there. Let him rock you. Let him think
you're giving him his head."
He taught me how to turn a herd,
to recognize a good bull, to irrigate a field.
When I was thirteen, he said I was ready
to pick a cow pony for my own.

We drove out to see her at the trainer's.
The fence around the long corral was studded
with scrawny local boys, waiving their hats and hooting
to see a girl mount up alone in the ring.
It spooked me and it spooked my green-broke mare,
who gathered up speed. I didn't know how
to be seen knowing how. Gave in
to her panicky, zigzag rhythm.
The fence rose up ahead, implacable as fate.

He leapt clear of the gatepost he'd been hanging on.
I saw his tough palm open in midair.
Time slowed down for him to grab my reins,
collect my boots, thrown wide from where I landed.
I felt the stillness in the dirt hard packed beneath me,
as he led my sweaty horse back around
to sniff and blow into my hair
and gave me a leg back up.

Kitchen Wisdom

In heart's gratitude for Mitzi

1950

I study you from the doorway. Your back's turned to me.
I'm putting off the moment I'll look you in the eye.
Our last cook bullied me: kitchen monster.
I am three years old and shy to introduce myself,
but Mommy is busy and I'm hungry for breakfast.

You face the stove, crooning a spiritual,
wielding a spatula. You have the upper hand.
When you turn around, you smile as if
we already know each other, you ask,
do I like my eggs sunny-side up?
Right then I become somebody
who likes her eggs sunny-side up.
You sit down across from me across the yellow Formica,
drink your Sanka while I run my fork across the runny yoke.
We're a team now, refugees
from the chill of perfection
out beyond the kitchen door.

1956

There's mother, leaning back against the kitchen counter,
her eyes lit with an unnatural glare.
She wants to penetrate me,
brand my heart with her words:
You will never have to do anything,
darling, that you don't want to.
Not in this world. Never.

She's talking out of her crazy place.
I know enough to ignore her,
but I'm scared that her words
have a snaky power to infiltrate.
The way she loves me, she wants to pull me
back out of life. To curse me with the myth of privilege.
I'm afraid that somewhere down inside I'll believe her.

You stand at the sink washing up,
your back to us. Just another appliance.
But the moment Mother's out the door you turn on me,
pointing your dishrag right into my face,
like a mother bear, growling:
You have to piss and you have to die,
and don't you forget it!

1965

Once my crazy mother dies, my father
marries hastily. A tight socialite
who brings her own stuck-up French maid.
Kitchen tension. Household tremors.
Twenty years of breakfasts
across the Formica table,
and just like that, Mitzi and I
go our own ways.

1967

Here I am, a student hippie from Berkeley
visiting Mitzi in her rundown old-folks' hotel.
We drink Sanka, she tells me jokes from TV,
and then we go out for sweets.

We are walking down Market Street,
Mitzi with her home permanent and blunt high heels,
I with my curtain of long hair and sandals.
Slippery sidewalk. She wobbles and lurches
and down she goes. I can't catch her. Passersby veer off.
She's on her back on the wet sidewalk.
I'm almost on top of her, pulling her up against me.
We sway together, mirrored in the department store window,
like a single thick bear rising to her hind feet.

And this shock of sex runs right up through my core.
It assaults me and warms me up and I take it in,
let it bathe me and restore me. Just like that.
Does she feel it? Neither of us would say out loud.
There we go back up Market Street,
leaning hard against each other,
laughing, as she would say, to beat the band,
up against a light rain.

Trajectories

Redondo Beach, 1962. The surfer band played a pretty good "Wipeout"
from the bed of a cherry '50s pickup pulling up on the high school lawn.
Cocking their heads as they rose, fingers twitching
and tapping a tight wail of notes
out of a sea of wires, speakers, snare drums, and steel guitars.
"Bitchin'," mumbled the redhead with teased hair
and tangerine lipstick. "I'm stoked."

Too fresh to the scene
to know how to posture, I stood and watched
Hank Crane lean his skinny hips out from grasshopper-long thigh bones.
Inventing angles that must have been mystic mathematical coordinates
to hold him up at all. Hinting at trajectories that took off into forever
through the technicolor California blue.

Lackadaisical, meticulous. Joint bones rotating off each other.
His attention inward, true to moving starting points,
a discrete conflagration of space and rhythm,
edging into flight.

Plenty of hotshots and showoffs strutting their moves
out on the bright green ocean around him, but I don't see them,
not now as I pull into the driveway,
as old as his mother must have been back then,
too worn out to haul groceries out of the family van.

When I hear the first bar of the Beach Boys on the oldies station,
I don't remember anyone in that cool crowd
except for Hank, a boy I never even had a crush on,
tethered to the swelling ground through balance and breath.
I stretch my calf out of the door at a new angle
and reach deep into it, ready to take a chance.

Off Redondo

My place was there, beyond the breakers
where the red tide bloomed in late summer,
streaking the paths of my fingers phosphorus.
My patch of ocean drawing me out
beyond the lip of beach where schoolmates
oiled up and danced the surfer stomp
to Jan and Dean and the Beach Boys.

I started my passage digging my toes hard
into the wet sand as the first ripples
circled my ankles with bone-gripping chill.
As I pushed on, my calves and thighs grew thick
and strange to me, alien extensions
plowing me forward till an upsurge
toppled me and I surfaced spitting,
a horizontal creature, blowing and stroking and whole,
thrashing toward the skyline where dolphins pinwheeled,
stopping just short of their domain.

I never knew how I knew it was the place, but I did.
The right latitude between land and horizon,
specific vault of ocean, a wet locale
where I hung like a sea blossom lolling in the swells,
angled, a loose stem, feet asway
above the silty, kelpy floor.

I find myself back in Redondo. It's thirty years later.
The old shake bungalows that sidled up to the beach
have given way to concrete high-rises.
But when I stroke out, the vast wet under-hall still holds me,
the cold and wet and salt and sky

coax me into something other,
all thoughtless sensation, moving just
to stay in place in the current. Becoming wave.

Chiffon Valentine

For my mother

Mother and I had shopped our way down Wilshire
looking for the right prom dress.
Our feet hurt, it was past teatime,
and I was tired of confronting my baby fat
in too many dressing-room mirrors.

We were starting to snap at each other
when I pulled out the chiffon gown.
Coral-hued, finely pleated.
I slipped it over my head and let it
slide down my hips, cool and languorous.

I turned sideways for her to zip me up,
halfway expecting the zipper to catch on too much flesh,
but it didn't, and we turned together to inspect
the girl in the mirror, widening our eyes
at the woman gazing back at us.

Her skin glowed against the coral.
Her breasts rounded high into the heart-shaped bodice,
and her waist sloped down to the span of a grown man's hands
before her hips angled out and the fabric
fell like water to her feet.

She could have emerged from the ocean
on a half-shell, so luminous
she filled the room with the light given off
by a creature in its first moment of being.

The three of us held each other's eyes
in an instant that reeled itself out and out
until I broke it, exhaling, stuttering now.
I couldn't wear this dress to my junior prom.
I was just sixteen and those jocks and surfer boys
would be too scared to ask me for a dance.

Mother fought me, but I was adamant.
We gave the apparition one last look
and I chose the pale blue silk,
slightly stiff with the straight-across bodice.

When I miss my mother I remember us
stunned and gazing, side by side,
and how she wanted to call forth into the world for me
all the beauty that opened itself to us
once in a dressing-room mirror.

On Not Being a Jew

For my brothers

Though I am, of course—
the legally adopted daughter of a Jewess.
Belonging, in this fold, passes down
through the matriarchal line.
Nevertheless, as a girl, I hid in my room
and held my face up to the mirror with family photographs
and prayed to a nameless god, in wild despair, for a trace
of my mother, wrapped in her Sephardic hauteur,
and of my father, the Ashkenazi mensch.

That wild despair itself was the first symptom of my Jewishness.
Adoptees, after all, are like Jews; both chosen
and dispossessed, we can't stop
calling out for the impossible homeland.
Calling for our origins—Eden, Israel—
it can't be reached on human feet.

But my own family thinks of me as a shiksa,
a generic California girl, eyes the blue of denim,
hair the glint of summer grasses.
Horses snuffle, hungry, at my crown.
The dark eastern strain, the stain of history,
is absent from me. I was chosen
as a piece of their escape, their dream journey
into the raceless freedom of their holy land.

So I gather recipes for the seder
while they perfect their California accents.
Still, each in our own way, believing ourselves the stranger,

we circle our inner deserts as we embellish our outward lives—
a Zuni bracelet, a quarter horse, a thesis, a poem.
We have our prophets—Shakespeare, van Gogh, Bashō.
We argue the finer points. That's how we know
beyond telling that we are one tribe to the death.

Bitter Chocolate

Mother loved her chocolate bittersweet. The bitterness
achieves a subtle force pushing up
the sweetness to where it blooms on the tongue.
She loved torch songs, grief offered up to the ear
by a voice determined to live it out.
She loved blood oranges, the smart crack
of the bat kissing the ball, Martha Graham's upward reach
planted staunchly in the ground.
How each voice wavers against its will
somewhere on the careful descent from high to lowdown
and comes back to itself on the other side of the chasm.

She did not love the crack in the sidewalk,
the false note, the scratch of ground glass mulling over itself,
the unkind cut, the unalloyed bitterness
of Seconal.

God, if you exist, you know this.
How could you let that pen touch down
on the prescription pad, let her doctor give her
a full bottle to prove that he trusted her,
my father spend the night in the guest room
to protect her from his snoring.
How could you let her children, asleep in their scattered houses,
fail to choke themselves awake on premonitions?
How could her water tap turn on like every other night,
her drinking glass not shatter, the floorboards hold,
the earth not throw us to our knees?

No, it will continue to revolve upon its axis
until her children's children and their children in turn
offer up their first songs to the changing light,
and I will not hear in their nascent sounds
the long reverberation of her voice.

Leaving San Francisco

For my father

We were a family then, and the sound
of the sea washed us hourly.
Now I am leaving, like a wave cresting:
The body of the ocean pulls me back.

Grown daughters keep a decent distance,
use discretion, change their names.
You used to coax me out of bed
on schoolday mornings. Unremarked upon,
the habits of a household grow extinct.

What are the innate pleasures poised
to fade into our backgrounds?
How we exalt in the lucency of this port town
where you've settled us. How it shines out clean
as white bone at sunset as we drive home
across the Golden Gate. The invocation of foghorns
intertwines our dreaming. We don't mention
how I won't be there, quiet and beside you.
I knew your heart when we lived in the same house.

On Earth

You can't step twice in the same river.
With a stone you can take your sweet time.
                           —Charles Simic

A child, I dug in the garden
For dinosaur bones,
Small red devils dancing,
China's moist brown underguts.
I told the little boy next door
To dig for scarlet three-pronged pitchforks.
He dug all day, and his mother
Spanked me for the lie of it.

And it's true, I wasn't quite
Expecting pitchforks,
And certain as a stone
Wedged in the old earth's armpit.
What does she cradle with gruff breasts,
Hoard between stone thighs?
(Like the secret drawer in my mother's bathroom,
Before I knew about blood.)

Is she bleeding, too,
Down in her darkest belly
While I call her Mother,
And dig at her?

She would not open her arms,
Secret earth-thighs, for my child's spade;
Instead she sang me lullabies
Of leaf-fall and graying mosses.

And I've been told there's metal at her core,
All ungentle to our soft flesh.
It's best we leave it there.
We rot and reappear from out
Her crusty skin, that's all,
Cling to her while she spins off song
Of wild lupine and squirrel bone.
And the best that I will ever do
Is dig a grave to lie in,
Only to reappear
Leaf-shaped in the spring.

Moon Tides

Loss of blood does weaken,
Life-will sickens,
Spirit overtaken
By waters of the moon.
Oh, there is something flowing forth
Beyond blood.

Women shut in darkened huts,
Away from eye-touch, sun-glance;
Bare curve of existence, like the
Moon on the wane. It was thought
Poisonous to behold them.

I suffer the poison,
Subtle turning back of life flow.
My earth ties rot, and I dream dreams
Of rolling on my back on the moon.
No strength at my hollowed center,
Body fading like a sap-dried leaf.

I seep out with each lost egg
Between my own spread thighs
And watch my body going on
Without me:
                    spirit losing
                            body losing
                                    earth.

But there are no dark huts here, too much sunlight, so,
Waiting for the ebb-turn of the moon tide,
Wanting ritual,
I buy myself a round white paper lantern,
Three bars of hand-dipped bayberry soap.

Naked Ladies

Didn't they just
rise up from the depth
of August's dirt when the heat
was stripped of nuance.
Like flappers, strutting their long,
smooth limbs, flaunting
garish, tinted faces.

They didn't come in flats from the nursery.
They crashed our genteel party of a garden
where each blossom
dressed its torso in cultivated leafage.
They unfurled without a by-your-leave
as summer panted its last dry breath,
too wrung out to stand guard.

These ladies smelled like Little Diva,
that cheap dime store cologne
I begged Mother to buy for me.
Its blatant odor offended her good taste,
and I learned why, one evening
watching my father water.
Hearing him chuckle low down with pleasure,
growl their naughty name and stretch
his long hose out to shower them
till they bobbed and swayed in the sunset.

An Unexpected Season

We leaf through Sunday's papers.
We doze and startle in the sun.
His bald head jolts forward,
then sways on its stem,
keeping him upright, submerged
in his dreams on the deck.
I am six. I memorize
each long hair bending and reaching
from his shiny, tanned scalp.

We leaf through Sunday's papers.
I am twelve, still free
to rub my palm across his silky dome,
catalogue each new freckle.
We doze and startle in the sun.

I am sixteen, running
from Mother's gulping rage.
to comfort myself in my new bed,
I call to mind those truncated snores
with which I watched my father wake himself,
having tilted too far forward.

I am seventeen when he awakes
to find her body, the empty
glass, the trail of pills.
My hand retracts like a claw, flinching.
We back off, each into the tangled
underbrush of our own shame.

I am nineteen. His new wife, a snapping
turtle, keeps me at bay.
I miss the scrub jay's rude squawk,
the red-tailed hawk's wide *cree*,
the turkey vulture's ancient, gliding silence,
and how we'd name them, call their calls,
startled from our dozing on the deck.

We leaf through Sunday's papers.
Nearing fifty, I notice
each solitary white hair scattered
Across his still-sleek scalp.
We wake up, still too shy for words,
and mimic the cries of unrecognized birds,
my father and I,
alone together after all.

Silences

It didn't matter what I did, actually,
as long as I kept my seams straight.
By the Summer of Love, I was challenging you,
swearing off nylons, bare toes in hand-crafted sandals.
You lowered your eyes. The gullies
running down your cheeks sank deeper.

So unlike the time you reached down
for the lever beneath my driver's seat
(you always drove) and straightened up
with my careless friend's
revolver in the palm of your hand.
Not a word—your eyes held me clamped
in the grip of your injunction:
"You will act like a lady."

And I did, Daddy. When it came right to it
I never smoked in public. And I addressed him as Sir,
the cop I flagged down, in my stoned haze, to rescue me,
lost in circles in our old neighborhood park.
I abandoned my protest placard to prod an old lady
out of the tear gas wafting down the college streets.
And when some cad would corner me, I'd lengthen my neck
like Grace Kelly playing a queen and stare right through him.
It worked every time.

I joined you on your death bed, holding you
steady in your morphine flailings.
I wore sweatpants, but still we danced
a formal dance. I followed your lead
but kept you turning toward me, through me
to the point where your silence
said *no*, said *yes* to all of it.

Parents

Theirs was not the usual *mishegas*; it never is.
She turned, on the blood tides of her mind,
into Medea thumbing through her cookbook,
Cleopatra conspiring with the asp.
He camouflaged his fearful exile's heart
in the stance of a rakish aristocrat,
swinging his umbrella, whistling,
"Mad dogs and Englishmen
go out in the midday sun."

Dinner a vaudeville affair, it was anybody's guess
which cues would be picked up, dropped.
Each one of us both prop and player.
Sometimes their disparate styles, in some giddy leap of faith,
would mesh over the cutlery and we'd gasp, suspended
in a web of flawless belonging. Held
by what we knew would never hold.

Now and then they'd slip their roles entirely,
and that's when I loved them best:
rediscovering their marriage dance
beneath the dark of the moon,
his fox's tail swelling out, her voice
as guileless as a floating loon's.

Call and Response

The famous psychic told her
she was a young, young soul.
Too young to concern herself
with learning the ways of earth.
Too young to look for the *no*
behind every *yes*.
She had no truck with numbers
or tying her own shoes.
She loved extravagantly,
and she thought that was enough.
She loved the bugs in the garden
she followed around on her knees.
She and her mother sang their love,
back and forth, call and response,
until a mockingbird took up their song
and no one knew for sure
who was professing love to whom.

BUCKEYES

For Francie Chouteau (1947–75)

Girls Springing

You had to stir me up at dawn. I kept spiraling
back into my pillow, into the opaque lull
of first light. But you sprang me, spurred
by your desire for sun against your skin.

Tracking and cornering obstinate cow ponies,
we mounted up and sauntered out the old corral gate,
hips rocking, bareback and easy
in old jeans and pointy cowboy boots.
We picked our way along the rimrock trail
opening into a half-moon circling
the foot of the farther hill.

Pale sun lit up the stubble of new spring grass,
the scatter of dawn-purple rocks,
our upstart chests. We tugged open
the mother-of-pearl snaps on our cowgirl shirts,
tossed them high across a mossy boulder edging the trail.
We kicked our horses, side by side,
up into a lope, a sprint, a lather.
Pushing off into the sunstruck, naked air.

We were a wave, four round-breasted creatures breaking
in a rhythm that broke us as one
into the untold pieces of the day.

Buckeyes

Today was a day for us: late August, the first buckeyes forming in their nubby pods. The skin, thick and tight-seamed, will wear thin and split by November, dropping fruit the color of a sorrel horse in the sunset. The fruit is dense and inedible, no human crop, but it felt so smooth, fit so well in our palms that one year we gathered hundreds, sorting them by size for the pleasure of touching and holding.

The wind comes up stronger toward sunset as it moves us toward autumn. You remember what spirit catches the horses in this wind. We were eleven when we saw it first, climbing the hill with ropes for a bareback ride. Late sun turned the yellow grass red, the horses' coats shone, and the muscle work stood out beneath. The big dun that was so gentle reared all the way up, and they took up speed like a single wave, circling the crown of the hill. The ground reverberated; the rhythm came up through our soles.

The brown colt we raised up as a stallion was a yearling then; he died last week at twenty-one. I couldn't let him go without your knowing, so I dreamed you up to tell you. You repeated what you told me the last time I saw you: that I wouldn't love you if I knew what you were really like. Dreaming, I abandoned the civilized reserve that hobbled me in daily life. I took you by your fine strong shoulders and shook you the way we used to shake the buckeye trees: with all my heart and muscle.

I knew what you were like... together we learned how to read and count! I knew how hard you fought, how hard you slept, what would make you lie. What strengths and needs your gray-blue eyes denied, your torso revealed in your growing, and I watched you, your trunk elongating, your round calves stubborn to kick off.

You grew in a burst of animal restlessness, a sudden source of undomesticated power. Womanhood came hard with its pressure to seem yielding. You turned against the muscles in your calves, the breadth of your shoulders, the power of your form.

Once, after high school, our lovers away, we went out drinking. You still lived at home. We were dressing in your bedroom, and you turned to me: "Don't wear a bra." We stood together in your childhood mirror, two bodies not merely echoing but inspired by each other. Bare-breasted, arms around each other's waists, having come that far.

How could we betray them, our brothers, our classmates, the well-worn habits of our mothers?

Now I live in the foreman's house. Today, that big chestnut with the watch-eye got tangled up in the fence. I gentled him so he could free himself. I didn't have to appear helpless; there was nobody there to see me.

Today again I could not believe that you chose to leave this earth, knowing how you loved horses in the yellow grass, the wind coming up toward sunset, the time when buckeyes ripen and fall.

I would have taken them all on—our brothers, our classmates, our mothers' worn-out habits—to stand up with you now.

Or so I say. I say a lot just to keep talking, holding your attention. Making you up. Making it up to you.

Deportment

We were waiting for them to be over, those years that felt like a prelude; we were preoccupied with a longing for our lives. We wore starched white middies and scratchy blue skirts, and the matron in gray wool had us memorize the daily routine of the aristocrats in classical Greece.

Reading in a footnote that the women were kept inside their own courtyards, we never gave it much thought. We were working hard to keep our legs crossed at the ankles.

Dressing Up

Your grandmother's house was furnished in Chinese Victoriana, the dragon armchairs, turn-of-the-century West Coast upper class. A Chinese matriarch inspected us from her gold-bordered screen on the wall as we dressed for dancing school.

Stray puffs of scented talcum powder, the cool glide of cologne along our necks. We chortled, murmured to each other even though we were alone: *Do wear a…don't wear a…bra…nylon stockings…wear your hair in a twist…where's your mother's perfume?…I always like you best in Chinese silk.*

You were impeccable in your navy blue chiffon, your cerise silk with the mandarin collar, the simple statement, nineteen fifties San Francisco good taste. Your practiced smile, implying, "I'm sweet and I'm interested," lifted almost, at the corners, into a smirk. You danced every dance.

After-Dinner Coffee

It was 1969, the June of your wedding; your mother had cancer, your friends were on acid, the social stances were threadbare. You were engaged to the all-city swimming champ, who never said much. Your mother was bemused but relieved to see you settled in her lifetime.

I came home from Esalen to proceed you down the aisle, refusing to wear underwear beneath my blue synthetic bridesmaid gown. Your mother wore yellow.

She picked out our dresses, tried not to talk politics, served us coffee after dinner from her silver service. Crooking her little finger in sarcastic whimsy as she sipped, she'd address me formally: "Oh, Miss Mary, haven't we had good times!" We'd ignore the sound of her husband falling hard on the bedroom floor overhead. He hadn't come to the table for years.

You cried in bursts those weeks before your wedding; it seemed in poor taste to ask you why.

Tell Me a Story

Behind the house you bought with your husband was a walled garden. It promised to afford a quaint seclusion with its wooden gate, its brick fishpond and big, scarred cactus. I'd drop by some afternoons, and we'd retire behind stucco walls to smoke cigarettes or a joint, drink coffee or supermarket champagne. Here, we hoped to drop our grown-up pretensions and treat our lives like novels, as we used to. Here, we envisioned leaning back into our own laughter, the sunlight spilling across our faces.

As it happened, the sunlight felt thin on our faces and we talked too fast, inhaled too often, strained to impose a humor that wouldn't take.

I brought your little boys tadpoles from the country. You fed them with frantic enthusiasm, but soon they rose, bloated, to the pond's surface. You bought a chicken, and then a rabbit. They liked to nestle together among the diapers on top of the clothes dryer. You noted their affection sarcastically, trying to reduce it to a mutual need for body warmth, teasing yourself with the hope that it might be more.

The chicken took sick. You kept it warm in a cardboard box on top of the dryer, reported its progress daily over the telephone, and buried it secretly at night while the rabbit slept. By morning, the rabbit was huddled, flat-eared, on the new grave.

You told me that story over and over. In the end it became your only story. Fur and feathers. Friendship, death, and mourning.

The Bridge Across

1962

"Oh, no," your mother said, "you may not
go to the hop with Moose and Charlie.
They live across the Bay." She invoked
"the Hump," a temporary construction anomaly,
a mound in the roadway that traversed all four lanes.
"We can't trust boys to drive safely across the Bridge."

Her diction rang out so precise it was a parody of herself,
but she was serious. I imagine Moose, that
teen colossus striding down the beach.
The wind comes up from behind and poofs
his greased hair into a chrysanthemum.
His chest is broad and rounded out
like Alley Oop's, the caveman on the hit parade.
I think with my palms. They want to follow
the curve of his muscles and meet behind his back.
Your mother thinks with her fear.

How does she frame the problem?
As geometry? Halfway through the tunnel
that intersects the island,
which is encircled by the Bay,
which is bisected by the Bridge,
runs an asphalt hump. Maybe she sees it mythologically,
a piece of local lore: Almost every weekend
another drunken seaman spins out
into the vortex of arcs and angles, skids, flies,
lands in the hospital and on Sunday's back pages.

Housewives cluck over their coffee.
Your mother rests her cup. In her mind's eye,
Moose and Charlie sprout sailor's caps as white as her saucer.
"No." She arches her eyebrow, mocking her own stance.
It annoys me how much I love her.

Or try psychology: for *hump* read
something swelling hard against a zipper,
the awkward resurgence of a mother's girlhood memories.
Sociology: Consider the unstated class distinctions that split
a mechanic's son from a lawyer's daughter at the end of summer.
Read the question: Can anyone make out the lines in the road
after too much beer and rock 'n' roll?

But what did we know? The day I got my driver's license
we bought a road map. Without your mother showing us
or telling us or even knowing where we were going,
we launched ourselves. A straight shot. Wind making
music in the cables. Just follow the lines, and we are arching
out across wide water, through blue air.

1969

Your mother was taking years to die, and it was only
on the long, dark span across the Bay
that I could let myself know it. Only when I drove, suspended
on that jeweled illusion flung between land masses,
did the the truth reveal itself to me:
They were dismantling her, breast by breast,
unhinging the womb of the woman
who had lived along the straight and narrow.
And though she had mocked herself for it,
that was the crux of her love: stubborn determination
to construct a web as forthright as that bridge
to raise us up above the currents and carry us home.

But nothing bore her up or over
as they carved the mainland of her torso into islands.
Driving the Bridge alone at night, too fast,
I still talk to your mother,
choke out the awful truth:
I will never be whole without you.
You were fierce in your craft of mothering.
Your raised eyebrow, the breasts you bargained with and lost.
But the Bridge, after all, goes nowhere.
It never mattered whether we went to the hop
with Moose and Charlie.
Or how fast I drive. Or how hard I dance.
The Bridge is a long reach, an altar
where the wildness that knows us and dissolves us
comes to sing.

Dawn Drift

The alchemy of rubber gloves,
of pomegranate seeds
and chicken fat does not suffice,
though in dreams I call them up
and let my fingers drift among them
to pick out, like a child on a piano,
the innate musculature of a song.

The cat paws me awake
as my thoughts still grope
for the fourth ingredient:
a sliver of garlic or a trowel
from someone's mother's garden
or the juice of a chicken,
simmered and chilled to a consommé.

I keep on assembling pictures,
the way I did when I was sleeping,
from myriad objects,
that I might choose well, stir them up, intone
the precise spell to make it coalesce.

Around daybreak, I understand the nature
of two spiritual elements I can almost name,
round and pearlescent, flowing between liquid and solid,
that I must combine in the proper stillness,
empty of any restless hope, but watchful
as they slide together down the thread of dawn.

My long-fingered cohort is weaving me a bridle
for the black horse that crowds me out of bed.

But his pawing turns into the cat's claw, roughs up my cheek.
I turn my head away, and now I rummage
through images, scraps, and syllables.
Feeling my way back into
the world when it was almost whole.

Losing You

Veering off the ambling road
onto a smaller lane, afraid I'm lost,
dusk coming on fast. Scrub willows
on my left disguise a roadside ditch.
A yellow highway sign pokes up: FLOODS DURING STORM.
Why do I resent it, the terse, flat language,
the being told at all? "Damn right, it floods!" I mutter,
as if I can feel the roiling water creeping up my leg to my thigh,
as I sink in, a tight mesh of branches clutching at my boot.

It hasn't rained since May, and it's been
thirty years since you mocked my determination to protect you,
best all-around girl athlete, homecoming queen.
From what? Unforeseeable traps like this ditch?
It was this ditch then, pounding with storm,
hidden by wet branches.
my sports car nosed down in, and you,
too drunk to disengage your mind
from turmoil, thrashing, wet leaves slapping,
your laughter choking up tears and dirty water
and something more,
as if this small flood pried open
a more dangerous chaos inside you.
The sound pushing out of it drove an icy
dread into my chest.

"We're safe," I screamed. "Stuck in shallows."
And I, the clumsy one, hauled you back out.
We braced our shoulders against metal, heaved,
pushed the car back up. And no one ever knew,
except me, who chanced in my later life

on the same obscure curve,
knowing for sure I'm not lost now, the way
I knew that you were lost then.

Silk Slip

You hold it out to me, gift
from a dowager aunt, cradled
in translucent folds of tissue you peel back,
bringing to the light its sheen, its intricate lace trim.
On the eve of your wedding, it taunts us,
calling up everything we're sure you'll never need again.
And so it goes. Handed off to a cousin.
No frills in the future we foresee
befalling you.

At your wedding, your mother
makes her last social stand,
good breeding holding her erect within
the delicate web of malignant fractures
that filigrees her bones.

Your father stays home with his bourbon, tumbles
down the first-story stairs as I lead you
down the aisle to the side of that stranger,
that good-natured, well-muscled boy-of-few-words
who used to camp across the river
from your summer cottage where we sprawled,
lazed in dry heat, unleashed
from the city's decorous restrictions.

We'd watched each other's trunks stretch out
like springtime cuttings, learned new girl games:
to shave our calves smooth, burnish
our bodies with rays of sun and coconut oil,
to creep through the house on moony nights
out to the beach, a secret tonescape
of mute and shimmer.

You took it in, the pale light glinting
off the whiteness of his teeth, the sand rotating beneath you.
Its silken surface was as cool as the water lapping its edge,
till you burrowed deeper. Then
the last stirrings of that day's heat eased you in, as warm
as his palm pressing down against your shoulder.
As warm as cool, as bright as shadowed,
as wet, as gritty, as sear, as silken. It wrapped you
in a sensory assurance, safe,
the way we felt wrapped in our silken slips
beneath our first formal dresses.

Safe, and you want to stay there.
Enough to leave home, that sudden carcass
of what used to hold you. You hold out to me
that slip, a sacrifice to possible.

We imagine no place for lingerie in your future
as a swimming coach's wife, drawers stuffed
with diapers and hand-me-downs. I let you
let it go, too appalled
by that vision to work my instinct
up my throat, to speak: Keep it anyway, hold it
against your breast, remember
that you are you, not just some
orphaned wife shoved into a bungalow
any more than you were just
some glorified prom queen. You are the girl who
slides your palm across your midriff for pleasure,
who rises out of the sun-struck water
on one ski, yelping to feel the raw life surge
through your arms, your glistening
getup of bones, to pass back into

the hard, wet surface. You, conduit for joy,
slanting your path to crisscross the boat's roily wake.
Sprouting from your own strength as you
bear up on the water.

This silk, take it home to your new home and stretch it
across your boy's hard belly. Do not give away
your right to feel, to writhe. Bring the river, bring the prom
into your new bed. Wake up
unknown rhythms between you.

My friend, do not walk head first into
that diminished vision that will lead you to open
your grandmother's medicine chest, to swallow
her pills, leave young sons orphaned, leave me
someone who has not been named yet,
neither widow nor orphan but a woman
who will never look forward without glancing back,
who wants to return to the river to immerse
handfuls of your ashes, rub them
into that creamy silk until it turns
dingy and soggy and sinks.

Ceremony

I felt that surge of girls and horses in the mounting pulse
of my fingers gasping at your coffin's lid, that
ceremonial door with no handles that, with no by-your-leave,
swung itself shut between us. Your body
stowed beneath a bulwark of chrysanthemums.

I was sure with both our hearts that I could
raise you in my arms and bear you
back up the aisle, lull you at the foot of the mother
oak we used to bow our heads to pass beneath,
rock you back to life in the next day's dawning,
the tight-bunched April oak leaves
stretching cramped spines and grappling to open
like your eyes newborn into mine.

At the mortuary altar, a creature
coiled itself inside me, silent and sinewy,
a stranger to the bestiary.
It gauged the weight of the wood, the vigor
infiltrating my fiber, tensing me to fling off
whatever foul, mistaken barrier
had presumed to erect itself between us.

The rumor of your death, the coffin, the awkward
shuffling mourners whose roles were played
by our own bewitched schoolmates and relatives.
We could shake them off like we'd gotten around
those silly schoolyard rules and curfews. I knew it.
The silence stuttered, wrapped me around.
I braced and curled my fingertips
up under the rim of polished wood.

But I had a husband back then who knew me, and knew better.
More stealthy than any beast, he leaned into me.
Lovingly encircling me,
he pinned my arms against my sides.
Reality. Propriety. I've submitted to their hold.
But the beast that leans its heart against mine
still longs to feel the give of that door lifting off its hinges,
to shatter the spell of this world acquiesced.

Coda

As new and shining as a birth—your going.
I would have borne and raised you for your company.

THE SHYEST, LONGEST LOVE

A Ripening

It was young like "the first time,"
it was timid like grass:
how it was.
Like young elephant glances:
how it was.
Like writing names in the water
with tulip petals, it was.

Now the elephants are tired.
They are walking, two by two,
down dusty roads toward sunset.
We are left in the jungle, crouching,
our love set out between us
like pears. Like ripe figs.

And it is, with us, the passion of wet leaves
clinging to tree bark in a summer rain.

There Was a Haven

There was a haven
In the beginning,
In your laugh.
And I was tossed,
Bright-colored, in its midst.
And later, in your eyes
That seeped beneath gay hues
And reached the petals of my dreams.
And finally, in your arms.
I hid my face against you,
A blown and quivering flying thing,
Found harbor in your warmth,
And you touched my soul for a moment,
Held it from the endless sky
Where once its keeper was the wind.

I would have blossomed
Had you held me longer.
I felt in me the bud
That would have flowered
Through the world
Until the sky was choked with petals
And the wind—no more.
I would have blossomed
Had you held me,
But now the wind—it lifts me,
And the sky is wild and cold.

Forgive me
If I call to you a little,
If I bruise your heart,
But too soon my pale voice
Is lost in wind.
And what then?
For I've forgotten how to fly.

"Call Me But Love..."

When we got down to it, you know, it was lonely.
We didn't quite play Romeo and Juliet
On that suburban, wife-swap-style set.
We played fuck.
We'd forgotten who each other was.
Mrs. Peach and Mr. Jones who wandered into the wrong
Bedroom on their knees. And fucked.
She thought he was the one she'd seen
At Stu and Sally's
With that wild purple tie, last Thursday.
She thought she was his wife.
Who cares what she thought?
It was me, wasn't it?
Rolling on my back on the guest-room bed?
I might as well have been in bed
With the president of Standard Oil,
And he with Martha Mitchell.
No, oh no, nobody at all.
He'd rather have been in bed with
Nobody at all.
You see, we'd forgotten
Who each other was:
Stained names on an old, thrown-out tablecloth.
Crawling, we'd turned the wrong corner
Of some obscure building-block world and met
In that old primordial
Nursery school in the sky.

Poem for Allen

It used to be serious, wanting you:
I'd feel out where you were in the room,
Reach for your hand instead of the hash pipe,
Blow my cool; offend your wife;
Get used to looking down.

And, well, I'm older now,
Used to needing less, learning to take more.
When you kissed me goodnight in the kitchen,
I barely looked up from the poem I was reading.
When you left the room, I was thinking
About snow.

I love you like an old, warm habit,
Like the falling leaves.
Someday we'll fall together
Like the leaves, loosely.
You'll take me away from some poem I'm reading,
And when you're gone, I'll remember
To think about snow.

Lingerie

Leaning over the bathtub, washing out nightgowns: some of them nylon, some of them flannel, all of them worn. Glancing down at my stomach, I notice for the first time how it hangs: the stomach from a drawing of an aging artist's model. The look on her face is vacant. The stomach sags as if emptied.

And it has been; I'd seen fat for so long. Only recently, turning thirty, have I seen the corners of my wing bones, the details and limitations of my frame. If the stomach sags, it is emptied of a burden: of wanting to be a rock, a roundness.

But wasn't there a time when I was both defined and unweathered? And did anybody see me?

Here in the afternoon bathroom light, a memory begins to breathe: sheer white cotton, nearly transparent, with pale blue stitching at the sleeve.

I took it off twelve years ago. It was dark in his bedroom. His parents were away. Standing in the glow of the streetlight, I felt naked in a sense the dulled world had ceased to achieve: a luminous heart beating through a transparent torso. I presented to a boy with flint-colored eyes a body that had never been looked at with desire. Turning to the side, looking down, I could feel his eyes move across me like a texture.

That was all. He preferred teasing to touching. Letting the silence settle down around us, he turned and walked out of the room; the door shut gently behind him.

I put on my clothes; eventually I put on my fatness. Through the reliable ordinariness of time, I haven't taken on my life. Now, I move deliberately from bathroom to basement; rummaging through boxes, I find that old white nightgown and toss it on the rag pile.

And later, watching my lover use it to clean the oil paint off his brushes, I consider this body he has coaxed back into the light. It wears the habits of my person: worry lines, sun spots, the fretwork of a woman's aging hands.

One Flesh

Picking our way over rocky outcroppings arguing:
What's yours, what's mine, how to move
this newly married body.
Just spring, clouds pulling out of
that vast, expanding blue that gives us
room to stretch and breathe in.
But still we slouch and drag our booted feet,
two knotted figures grumbling across the horizon,
that slash of space that tree frogs fill with croaking.
Between us, wild iris push up through volcanic dirt.

Still trudging, I glance down into
the rough streambed we're crossing,
almost dry now and smoothed in places
by the iridescent lichen that feeds
on thin spring light. I stop my glowering,
clamber down among small boulders, find
a moss-encrusted hollow to cradle me,
laugh: a voice that spirals out of rocks.

Your body swivels toward my call,
these rocks, the water they have held.
You're sucked down in and peel back your anger,
our wools and denims, press our skin
against the light that strikes the living stone.

We belong to the cries that clamor through us
to earth, sounding the season
between winter-water run and dry creek bed.

The Mercy of Marriage

Toward the end of a winter's afternoon
spent riding long waves of love,
I return to the bed blowsy with pleasure
and hold out to him a bottle of sparkling water.
A sneer gouges the lines around his languid mouth
into unforgiving grooves: "With all that wedding crystal,
is it too much to expect to drink out of a glass?"

I shudder. The open arc of my perception
spirals down to a spotlight, focuses in
on blue and yellow plaid. I want to tear
those damned, complacent pajamas off his back.

I leap upon him, sink my teeth
into those seams, which prove too much for me
as does, of course, my husband,
rising up in the delight of his animal strength
and pinning my arms behind my back.

I flail, ranting as he drags me
into the bathroom where he offers us up
to the wall of mirrors: "Look at yourself!"
His teeth are clenched
in an effort to hold and not hurt me.
I see myself, slit-eyed, spitting homemade curses,
and I see him smirking
on the verge of taking joy in shaming his lover.

Time and space converge to hold us while the mirror
deconstructs us into planes.
We stand in a timeless vault of light,

reassemble ourselves around our living eyes,
search out and receive the other,
the one we've said yes to.

Settling Up

My skin recalls your touch, slow-burning
embers flaring, dying, blazing up
along an unexpected limb.
You moved in and out of the room like a mood
or a play of shadows, and if I tried
to name you to myself as an animal,
a young buck fading back into the brush was as telling
as a mountain lion crouched in summer's grasses.
My own hesitation captivated me
when I was young enough to believe that instinctive
startle might be love.
Once you had gone, I would imagine you out there,
elusive, maybe free. The mythic cowboy, roughing it for me.

You'd show up off season, between cattle auctions,
rodeos, traveling carny shows.
Seeking refugee from a scatter of baffled girls,
hardened ex-wives and scrappy kids petering out behind you.
With each return you'd proffer, reverently,
as if it were a gift, your new tattoo
or latest scar from a bull ride or a bar fight.
Age never matured, it distorted you.
You circled in on yourself, bewildered
by your own simple pain.

Still, I liked to conjure you riding
the far fences of the backcountry
as I stood late at night doing dishes over the sink.
I'd squeeze my left hand to remember,
down in its webbed bowl of muscles,
the fierce, reined-in joy of streaming,

like a low-flying hawk,
across long expanses and up warm rises:
loving a territory, a familiar wild.

Now you have limped back, a bloated
boy-hero gone to seed, your oversized truck
towing a battered horse trailer that cradles
your Harley, your guns, stale bedding.
You have parked it all on my leafy street.
You want to root your broken body
to my kitchen table. Muscled knot of pain,
you've been imagining that what I've made out of my life
could be called home. You want to fix
my sagging gate and be needed.

Involuntary Motion

Falling into Bed

What am I doing on my feet up here, stoned and straddling
the body of my big-boned, quadriplegic lover,
my own legs raising me high up
beyond where he could ever go?
I look down, as if soaring, onto ridges of ribcage,
craggy face, blue-eye pools, spreading streams of hair.

I hover over him, giddy with height,
until, shamed by my own joy,
I feel my balance start to waver,
then lurch. He stares straight up at me,
unable to move but registering
my every shift and shudder.
Unremitting, he marks the instant
I lose control of the surge of my own motion.

His torso ripples with the same waves
of involuntary motion that inspire our lovemaking
but cannot protect him now
as I fall, full out, on top of him.
He turns his head away from me
with an amazed and knowing snort.

We lie splayed out against each other.
The silence swells between us, conjuring
a mood even we cannot fathom,
until the stillness convulses.
Imperfect and as one,
wc laugh out loud.

How What We Had Had Us

The next time I find myself
straddling his long, sprawled body
I let my rocking pull me to my knees,
my pelvis docking up against
an outcropping of hip bone,
where I lull myself, as willing as seaweed
riding the skin of the surf.
The first wave coils in the pit of his belly,
hurls him up against me.

I'm caught on the swell,
the surge heaving through me,
crashing my inner gates,
flooding the bowl of my pelvis,
mounting the spiral of my spine,
till I become the wave's crest,
rollicking, breaking over him,
my face tumbling down
into the hollowed cove of his shoulder.

I can't stall the pounding,
can't breathe in enough air
to feed the laughter that convulses me.
In a desperate ploy, I tap my index
finger on his shoulder blade,
willing this rogue energy
back into his body, and it works.
The force recedes back into him.
I collapse against him,
clutching his biceps.
My gut feels his torso start to ripple.

The swell builds, fiercer, wilder,
till he chokes on his own laughter,
taps his finger on my shoulder,
and I'm caught once more, thrashing,
gasping for breath.

Ice Ages

I

I left when I couldn't get
back to you and you were standing right
in front of me in our living room
where life stopped cold,
our feet still planted
on what had been home ground.
Your words rose like steam
into frost: "Don't do this!"
I was frozen out by the absence
in my own chest. I couldn't get back to myself,
and you were calling, calling
from three feet away into the glacier.

I felt myself misshapen, all eyes, no mouth,
no sense of touch to find us in this blizzard
that annulled us in our home as we stood
knee-deep in it, and you doubled over
before me on the hardwood floor
and you howled, as animal
as I was ice.

(1982)

II

Yesterday, forgetting it used to be our anniversary,
I woke up halfway into a poem about
your oblong-printed fingertips.
As I wrote, I felt them reaching
back for me, our ghost limbs.

That amputated clasp that keeps on
feeling for its own faint pulse.

The phone: an old friend telling me
how your next wife, not me,
but the good one who kept the table
and the bed linens folded separately
and the children tucked in safely down the hall,
is frozen out of herself as we speak
by the tumors threading, glacial, through her brain.
And I doubled over, screaming
backward down my throat and
through our canceled living room,
the permafrost of facts.

Your howling reaches me again
in the aftermath that never ends.
Tell me, do you still look up
into the corner of your eye when you need to
slip into your other, silent world?
Look up there now, you'll find me,
that blue that hides itself
deep in the core of ice.

(1999)

Adultery in Late Middle Age

Your arm lifts and settles, rattling the ice in your glass.
Dusk, and the mottled flagstones around your pool
give up their heat to our recumbent bodies—
the heat of a desert day edging into autumn.
Here's time enough to watch the first star bloom.
We dawdle, our feet barely touching,
back from love at the Aloha Motel.

I imagine the warmth seeping up through your wing bones
as I feel it penetrate my own. How unlike
the way I felt the first time, my young skin tingling
as you tugged at my sweater to pull me down;
all I could think about was falling into your kisses,
not your boyish unease with my outright hunger.
Always filching scraps of time. Always cheating.
You couldn't ever choose me or renounce me.

In the kitchen, your second wife drains the pasta
(we can hear her shake the colander),
deceived by our low-key friendliness.
We don't flaunt passion or waste time berating each other
for not having wanted the same thing at the same time.
We just let ourselves unfold, like now,
when it's too late but our bones still pull together,
and we discover something new: We both know the lyrics
to every Broadway show tune. Our raspy voices fill
the burgeoning night. Out of tune and out of season,
but I feel so gay, in a melancholy way, that it
might as well be spring…

Fidelity

It is not so much the vow as the ongoing
listening for the slightest
strum or shiver to announce itself...
that unbidden eddy in the underground spring
that joins the pelvis to the heart.
To give it one's steadfast attention
so you know with canny certainty,
as it rises from the pulse to the surface of the skin,
in just what secret plain or hill or thicket
in the known wilderness you live beside
it arises from. The willingness
to allow your singular body
to dissolve into a current, a simple current
in the ageless river of desire.

First Passion

Put it down gently;
this toy is old, it has been handled
by the eager-fingered children
of all people. Each one is certain
(s)he is the first to make it breathe.
Each one is right.

Free Fall (Whiteout)

It was winter, and the waters
pounded through the rocks,
gathering force, dispersing.
I stood stock still, observing
your ashes fall from my brother's fist
down into the ravine: white flakes,
then the sudden chalky segment
I thought must be shin.
Unembellished,
exposed in free fall.

This moment holds: white bone
as familiar an intimacy
as your body's ritual lowering
into your bath each evening, your ankle
breaking the water's skin, the crust of bubbles.

White skin, white tub, white bubbles: the sound of running water,
of the waters running off the earth again,
gathering force. You and I
came here often to listen to these waters
that have taken us up, dispersed us.
We are long gone on their currents.

On the Day We Used to Call Our Anniversary

I was pulling up words with my tongue
in the dawn, out of the silt of dreaming.
My crotch and belly and face were wet and salty,
and I was struggling to tell myself what I couldn't forget:
those swirling ridges indenting the tips
of your fingers, which are wide and flatten out
into planes that smoothed against mine
in the sanctuary of the theater's dimming light
or pressed up, bubble-haloed, to measure
themselves against mine in the bath.

My cheek still knows the imprint
of your whole hand as it struck me that time, goaded
by the sharp-beaked words hurtling out of me.
Your hand shifting down on the gear stick to a full stop,
intersection of Market and Castro,
while your left hand clutched and unclutched the wheel,
knuckles whitening, till it lifted off
and came down slant across my stiff, I-dare-you sneer.
The caves of bone resounded in my skull.

Two decades have layered up musty webs
between our fingertips, those heat sensors seeking
each other through the rain forest of sheets,
the museum's serious silence, the dark subterfuge
of laps beneath the family table. We spoke
with our fingers, and all our words—
those words I kept insisting on—
inept stand-ins for our hands.

These days I have your number, and we've settled on
a language that glances off everything we know.
We even shake hands now and then, though it's
easier to hug, and we never lift our fingers up
to feel their fine hum rise between us. I would
follow it anywhere, and here, in my new life that I
inhabit more comfortably, to be sure, even now, if I let it,
my palm angles outward, fingers trawling
the currents of sleep for your touch.

(re)birthing

You are in love with sex and sleep, after the lull of sex and sleep, the wet skin that encloses my skin. Do I know it as separate, have I been warned by a cramp or pinch that it moves separately? What was me becomes a blanket of flesh, my sleeping bag, slick and warm, becomes a muscle, a different will, molding, pushing me down, my crown into the opening of the vortex, rolling me down and the muscles inside me, a dance, a corkscrewing, calling within my muscles to work, turn, turn, work the way, it is not separate, the holding, kneading insistence, it calls up a will in my muscles, pressed hard against and working, working.

I give my wholeness to the pressing and coiling, to meet it. I know how (how?), it requires of me only work, will, intention, and then I slip out, am free of, open up into. The agony of pulling in the air.

And then hands, fingers, palms swarm over me. Did I give them permission? I need, I need a returning, the returning of my flesh to the mother's, my skin, my ears, to the beat that returns me, the beat of her heart and mine answering against it. Return to what I later call myself, my other, my God, the turning back again to the beating.

Over and over again.

Sleep, sex, singing the thread of sound in my muscle's memory.

Breastplate

how did she come by this
breastplate of blue ice molded to her ribs
protecting her heart but leaving
her breasts exposed? sometimes she used her breasts
in her own defense, distracting the onlooker
from noticing the fierce, shy self beneath them.
peering. fumbling. needing to know.

her breasts, correctly managed,
could take up enough attention
to leave her invisible:
free to dig into the raw material,
the web of intentions uncoiling themselves
beneath the scrim of consensual reality.

to mark the unacknowledged:
the seducer backing her into the corner,
the shyster's eye sliding over the silver,
the snakeoil salesman coughing into his sleeve.
manipulation keeps passing itself off as love.

she even slept with people in order to evade them,
to keep them from tracking her,
her awkward, feral heart.
leaving her free to feel into wind over water,
river rocks taking their shapes from the current,
faults rubbing up against each other beneath her feet.
the fine attention of animals, the unexpected
kindness of a mother-in-law.
in the hills around capetown,
each species of stone cactus

matches itself to the slope it grows on.
the onlooker only sees different shades
of grayish or greenish dun.
until the perfect camouflage abandons itself to reveal,
one spring morning, a landscape of white,
each thumb-sized stone covering itself
in frilly daisy petals.

when she stands back far enough, existence
seems to be a nest of secrets, concealing,
in order to reveal themselves.
to make up yet another way to hide and then uncover.
if she let melt that fine blue ice
and let her breasts lie back against her heart...

Knives

She filled her bed with knives, he said,
to keep away the sadness.
Driving through thick hits of rain, opaque curtains opening up,
each one, onto the next. Suspending me
between serial flashes of blindness. I grope
for the knob on the radio. Listening helps me
find myself like rubber treads gripping asphalt,
not just water carving up space.
A human voice, stray words and phrases
hitch me back to my breath. I ride syllables, not images.
But the broadcaster, with his deep, neutral voice,
stretches out a sentence I cannot
deconstruct into arbitrary sounds:
She filled her bed with knives
to keep away the sadness.

The Shyest, Longest Love

You who hate to sleep have rolled
against my body and wedged your thoughts between
the bottom stones of the mind's dark river—
how often now across four decades
of seldom seeing each other.
And always mid-sentence.
Revving up into "Do you know how beautiful…"
or "Have I told you how I long…" your pulse
slows against my pulse to join it.

I watch over you as you float through
the deep dive you've taken into yourself.
Expanding into the silence, I become
the water, the mindless, observant fish,
the steady moonlight that holds us.
Settle myself in under the eerie weight
of the mountain's shadow, listen
to your fretting mind let go of itself.

WIT'S END

Diagnosis

"The bad news is, it doesn't kill you."
The doctor makes his little joke.
Fixing her eyes on the crystal miniatures
that inhabit one corner of the desk stretched out between them,
she coaxes her cheeks to release the grin
she'd feigned to meet his punch line.

She is there because her body
aches from her bones outward, she sleeps
in thirty-minute snatches, her stool
has turned the color of clay, and her skin's
a jaundiced yellow that requires a whole new wardrobe.
She finds herself forgetting where she is, where she's going,
the beginning of the sentence she's just finished.
She has technicolor nightmares and falls down in public.

The doctor utters, for the first time, her condition's given name:
Chronic   Fatigue   Immune   Dysfunction   Syndrome.
Disjointed string of words, a pallid
stab at what had entered her.
Blank-faced, he delivers the treatment plan:
"Lower the expectations for your life."

She pretends not to hear him.
Like the time she'd been beset by a roving gang
of drunken boys on a deserted street at twilight.
She'd kept her head up, walked on as if they didn't exist
and they'd backed off her.

But there's no backing off here. It is this moment,
not the actual instant when she'd failed to notice

the disease breaching her defenses, but this moment,
as the doctor looks right through her, that she crosses over
into the vast, unmapped terrain of the invalid.

Day-Bed Dozing

Disjointed images and dream shards
keep startling her awake:
She's down on her knees trailing June bugs
through the old kitchen garden;
eyeing trays of oysters bedded down
on shaved ice in a French café.
She's rubbing her fingers in the moist red soil
of Ohio cornfields and graveyards,
cooking paella, head bent into her husband's
as they watch the saffron bleed its stamens into the broth.
She's back in dance class, improvising,
smelling the musky odor of the wooden boards
as she rolls, rises, sinks back down
to roll and rise again. She's listening
to a client's dream. It's so articulate.

Her own dreams aren't messages to analyze;
they are splintering images
torn out of context and hurled back at her
from beforehand, from that bygone land
she considers real life. How can she wake up
and inhabit this exile? Breathe.
Breathe scraps of the past back into her body.
They're still living. Here. Remember.
How to sink down, to roll,
to rise up again.

Blaming

Wit's end... How did she get here?
Can a lie make you sick? Your own lie
you can't tell that you keep telling?
Or that bygone lie from somebody you trusted,
rancid by now, blown into this moment
by some trace on the breeze?

She puts down her cup, listens inwardly
to a voice edging away from what it's saying
even as it says it.

And that complicit aspect of herself
she can't stop kicking, the dog in her
that consented to believe and goes on consenting.

And the lie that was conceived in truth but distorted
by that treacherous translation into syllables,
or by the tilt of her head as she took it in.
The birth canal, the coil
of her inner ear, the netted pathways
through her cortex that form
and re-form every word.

How can she tell you what it's like, here at wit's end?
No source for the truth but that tuning fork
inside her now—that pitch she finds way after way
to turn away from.

Rituals

She presses her torso into the earth,
peels back in her mind's eye
layers of vegetation, strata of minerals,
down to the furnace at the core,
clamors down through the heart of it: "Heal me!"

Did her own lie make her sick? Kneeling
at the altar beneath the marble, middle-aged Madonna,
vowing only death, not simple outrage, would part them.

The contempt he'd imbibed with his mother's milk
seeped into her, opaque infusion
she knew she could not survive. Spat up her vows.

She presses her naked ring finger into the earth.
She stays a long time.

Workout

She bows to herself in the gymnasium mirror.
In dreams the gym looks like it does in life.
It is her person that has been dismantled. Her right thigh,
a plank of driftwood screwed into her hip.
Bones glow the creamy patina of a Dalí skeleton.

Her left leg is missing and the head of her crutch
tucks into the armpit where her arm is wound
onto her torso with electrician's tape.
Her head, a stitched helmet off a de Chirico canvas,
holds itself up with shaky poise.

She admires her own savoir faire as she works her way,
rocking, crutch to heel bone, into the weight room.
Lines up remnants of herself to a machine.
Steadies her spine to work the wooden leg.
It's the lifting that sets her all a-wobble.
Her head falls forward, and the first tears slide
out slit eye holes down the leather mask of her face.

Secret Agent

And that was years ago. Unlike the roving
band of boys, this menace
still accompanies her. Takes her down at will.

"What is it, really?" she pleads, year after year.
"We haven't pinpointed the causal agent,"
they keep saying, "but there is one, some virus or bacteria that,
combined with a genetic lapse in your immune system
and the degraded environment we all live in,
is able to keep operating." Cells and terror.
She feels like she's consulting the FBI.

The enemy can't penetrate
the miniatures on the desk with their crystalline structures
or the doctor with his hardy genes, but has infiltrated her,
set up house at the trunks of her nerve cells.
Taps his way as agile, as blasé
as Fred Astaire in a top hat, only eager,
with an evil-hearted lilt.

Yuppie Flu

I am tired of the turn
of every day into another, still enshadowed by
that illness with the innocuous name
that partners me from maturity into seniority,
drawing compromising circles all over
the map of what I can be.
"Here you can go, but no farther."
I am sick of its grabbing my muscles at just those points
where they widen into power, so that I stumble,
getting off the bus, into a stranger's arms.

And I am sick of the grief-struck
faces that slide across my gaze in dreams and retract themselves:
the children I could not have because
I was too tired; the husband
whom I pushed out, convinced that his double,
the one who cut swaths of gore through my nightmares,
was the real man. The real life
I thought I had some right to
all balled up and tossed out
by a being I cannot grasp who lives
inside the nerve ends in my fingertips and migrates
on the tides of my own circulation
across the blood-brain barrier into my thoughts themselves.

So who is speaking when I speak? Who inhabits
the occult chambers of my mind and deals the words out?
Sometimes it's him. Sometimes it's me. Sometimes
I imagine I know which is which.

Or I get ambitious, try to start
a dialogue. I can envision him all right,
nimble as Astaire and as cheerfully enthusiastic,
his fingers, techno digits working
the switchboard that controls my flummoxed cells.
I confront, I flirt, I implore. I cannot
get him to talk back to me.

It's the actual I am sick of, that this replacement
for family and work confounds
all reasonable expectations in my actual life.
Can I sleep, think, digest today?
Why not? Friends all say I look good
and think I'm lying, or they don't say
how bad I look and stay away.

Still, one season or another goes by well enough,
sometimes a year. I take up hope ferociously,
but I'm older every time and don't know quite how to act.
Fifty-four with a thirty-six-year-old's
interrupted ways. Ways of grasping
the context for some hunk of time in which
I'm granted well-being. Out of context. Out of line.
Out of patience. Still making it up, how to do this,
still, still bellowing: "Out, out, out..."

Waking Up on Disability

She wakes up frantic, yesterday's headache just
releasing its grip across her skull,
the vertigo winding down like a hula hoop.
Agitated by souped-up, boiled-down afterimages
of things she used to do before
weird illness ripped her out of the ongoing:

she and her best friend rustling through the leafy night
searching for lodging in the brown-shingled, riot-ridden town
where we really went to college once;
a '60s encounter group, people
she'd actually been there with and forgotten
showing up again to dig the wax
out of each other's ears with long and intricate utensils.

Fever and the cramps digging into
the long muscles down the back of her legs
will keep her home alone today,
like a child whose mother
has gone shopping and left her
with a pile of books and time.
Time unbound to float in for as long as she can.
Rocking lonely and afraid that its sheer mass
will pile itself up into the wave that finally
pulls her under.

Cyclic/Chronic

I was like you yesterday, walking to the post office,
paying my mortgage, dismissing
the rest of my money business,
and straying from library to coffeehouse.
Plundering a poem, plundering several
for their air, their meat, their surface
and covert intentions.
Drifting home at dusk beneath a half-moon, the first star,
through the summer wind.
A mood of belonging, insinuating safety
at least for the night.
But the eyes of my dreams shone with malice:
my neighbors, all got up in gangster suits,
sidled house to house, spitting hoarse words:
"No, no. We don't want you here!
There's a plot unfolding, and we don't want
your awkward stalling, your banging around to fit in."
The cat jumped off my bed and went
to sleep in some other room.
Hearing him, I wake to a climate of fever,
knotted in damp bedding, shoulder muscles coiling back
from whatever use I put them to in my dream,
from trying to find a way into
what I now need to find my way out of.
I want to go to bed, but I'm already here.

Indigo

Out of the flat pewter horizon
that without a self pulls to itself
tear-shaped liquid orbs, they
draw together from within into rivulets, runneling
as if sucked by a voracious mouth
into a mounting, spitting curl that spills over itself.
Impossible blue wave. About to flatten you, but no,
tumbling downward, it penetrates your fibers, snakes
into nonexistent spaces between your cells.

You forget to breathe, but it doesn't matter.
You are swept up, folded in,
alive, beyond breath and boundaries.
Thigh, belly, throat, thought
are threads of memory stripped of will,
part of an indigo transparency that nothing
called into being, least of all itself.

Tracking

I've been walking on a trail for a while, a good long time now. It's almost familiar, though I haven't walked this way before. The day is hot, I retreat inward, almost mindless within the ongoing rhythm rising up through my feet. There's a dip in the path and I come to a pond. It appears that the trail ends at its grassy edge, but no, I walk on in, the water cool, almost cold against my ankles, the backs of my knees, my lower parts and now my belly.

On I move, single-minded now as though discovering in my stride a commitment, an unforeseen loyalty to the path. Brackish green water laps at my navel, my ribcage, the delicate rims of my collarbone.

I wonder if I will go on giving myself as it bears upward toward my lips, my nostrils. My eyes remain relaxed and open, seeing with a bright new clarity into and through the water. I hope that my breath holds, that I will remain patient enough to emerge on the other side.

Winter Spill

A dream balanced on the lip of a cup
gathers itself into one final drop
poised to fall, me below in readiness
to catch it on my tongue.

Will it be the aftertaste of last night's storm,
or fresh milk honeyed
to remind me how, even now,
there is sweetness?

I want to know this dream.
I still myself, willing time to stop
until the cup upends itself.

But my breath is labored.
Time has turned stale.
While I was distracting directing,
the dream went on
to dream itself through:
while I was
the pleasure of a single drop
at play
on the lip of a cup.

CLAIMING KIN

He Lived as Though

He lived as though he were making it up to somebody.
A born misfit, too anxious and exuberant, taking on
everything that scared him, that he loved.
Farm boy to banker. Banker by day, protestor by night.
Then day and night, resisting, strategizing, cutting up
over avocado sandwiches. Talking spices
or poetry or outrage, elaborate curry dinners
cooked with his cool, dry hands. While he dreamed up
the Gay Men's Buddhist Group, the anti-nuke march
that I couldn't say right: Legs Against Arms.
But always as dapper in his good wool suit
as whimsical in street-theater masks or occasionally drag.
I once saw the mayor cross the street to shake his hand,
and Tibetan lamas, attended by monks,
stayed at his house when they came to town.
His ego ideal was Ferdinand the bull,
who turned his back on the bullring to snuffle
flowers beneath his favorite cork tree.
Flagrant, shy, and gracious.
Madcap yet sideswiped
by quaking, 3 A.M. dread.
Can you see him yet, How could you?
His attributes snap off and tumble,
brittle leaves circling his bare, ringed trunk.

But they elongate, these days of his dying.
His spirit opens out and basks.
I grip the phone as if I could capture the wonder in his voice.
"I'm losing pieces of memory," he tells me.
"I had to look up your number today. But listen:
I need to tell you: It doesn't matter, not any of it.

How hot is your sex life, is the pasta al dente,
sexism, patriarchy, war! I mean the President—
it doesn't matter. It's just what goes on."
I listen to a life of fear and love and work roll off his shoulders,
leaving joy so deep it's almost shameless.
Shameless.

Time takes a sudden swerve, and these days spin out into those.
Days I cannot enter. The number my fingers dialed by themselves
    for thirty years
"no longer in service." I riffle through photos, replay
your last message on my machine: "I love you dearly."
At his wake, we admit we all thought he was our best friend,
circle and take up the mic to tell his stories, to give him
back to each other. Even as we speak, he shatters
into other people's versions. The object of our affections,
he has left the room.

Claiming Kin

The boy was a passionate football fan.
Back home in the trailer in the Georgia pines,
he had crossed over into the occult realm of television sports.
The Dolphins were winning when electronic snow
dissolved the players. He scrambled up
to jog the antenna on the roof.

I imagine him as he pushes up out of his TV trance,
throwing open a door that gaped out
onto a landscape the tornado he had never
heard had ravaged: his front porch gone missing,
his buddy's bedroom perched askew on its foundations,
the shell of the next-door trailer flattened,
the old road itself demolished in the wind's raw path.

The neighborhood was vacant. Sunday
in a churchgoing town. Nobody
called out to him in pain or bewilderment.
His mother, that stranger who had once given me
a hushed-up birth and put me behind her,
sat wedged between her husband and her eldest son
in a pew in the Methodist church.
The boy unleashed the dogs and rambled,
a solitary witness, through the aftermath.

When we two met up, almost by accident, in mid-life,
and claimed each other true blood siblings,
he sat down and told me this story,
his way of telling me we saw eye-to-eye:
two initiates secretly skilled
in the practice of fitting the world back together
around an eerie silence.

Hosting Georgia O'Keeffe

Friends in-the-know had reservations
about inviting her to dinner.
She possessed a quick hand to accompany
her discerning eye.
Your squash-blossom necklace was safe, your Zuni pot.
But if you caught her palming your own special rock—
the black, water-rounded rock you'd picked up yourself
off the floor of what once was an ancient seabed—
she would explain how she needed it more than you did.
Her brush would transform nature into art.
The living image, reaching out from museum walls,
would offer itself up to everybody.

This rock she cradled in her long, famous fingers
would belong in the canon of New American Art,
one more facet of the nation dreaming itself up.
Georgia was America's own homegrown goddess,
tracking the crude, refining process
of how the people and the land
receive each other.

And I applaud her willfulness, I do. I want to.
Only I imagine the host navigating
the post-party silence. He's off-balance, missing the weight,
the cool round blackness that fit his hand just so.
My empty palm reaches out as if to give it to him,
but mid-reach it retracts and grips it for my own.

The Warsaw Ghetto on Late-Night TV

His cap is woven of wool, quality wool, the kind
they imported from Flanders in those days,
and his coat well cut above his cuffed knee pants.
Real tortoise-shell buttons, meant to be fastened by Nanny,
who polished the brass buckles on his leather sandals.
His clothes bespeak routine, comfort and civility,
fancy birthday parties and, when he's older,
lessons in the shul.

But the dance this boy dances out there on the curb
was not taught to him, neither for pleasure
nor for ceremony. He is making up every step.
Or drawing it out of some ancient store
of human necessity. He clowns, using every facial muscle
as if he's been schooled in begging.

And not to surprise Papa, come home
from a business trip on the long train,
or to bend close in and smell Mama's perfume,
enclosing himself in the rustle
of her petticoats as she dresses for dinner
and considers that the time is approaching
to teach him to bow like a gentleman.

Where is his mama as he dances?
Not in the grainy film clip I'm watching.
Where is his big-bowed sister whose piano teacher
said she had promise, whose ringlets
swung across her face as she played?
And what about Nanny, who buttoned and ironed
and sang her charges to sleep?

Can he wonder and still keep time?
And what about the cameraman who kept his stride
in the streets a-bustle with horror and smug satisfaction
long enough to shoot this mugging imp?
And the onlookers who don't notice
that this human puppet's joints are big and mobile,
his clothes whimsically baggy,
because he's starving?

They throw him a coin or crust because his charms protect them
from their own fear, from the horror
that jerks me awake on my warm leather couch. Caught,
sixty years later, imagining you or I could be safe.
Floundering: Do I have the right or obligation
to watch or to turn off the big eye?

In Another Country

My mother runs a souvenir stand alongside the rutted path to the temple of sacrifice. Throngs of people flow by her every day, and one day, one of them is me. I come as a pilgrim. Head bowed, I pass my mother by. I join the villagers who shuffle down the hill holding chickens to their breasts, dragging goats by fraying ropes. A cacophony of squawking, bleating dread.

A stranger, I am forbidden to enter the sanctum. I stand, polite and sickened, at the gates. Hear animal voices rise. Grow hoarse. Fall silent. I tell myself that my gods have no unslakable thirsts. Make no unseemly bargains.

The worshipers emerge. Their chests, their arms, are free now. Yet they do not look uplifted. They look down into the dust. Together, we trudge back to the surface of the earth.

There, I recognize my mother, a wraith hawking her death debris. Her thick black hair all matted. I haven't seen her since she died. When she looks into my face with her brimming hazel eyes, I want to fall into her arms. She is mute. She picks from her table a long bone, maybe her own. She holds it out to me.

I still carry that bone. I have given it a charcoal face. Stone beads. A horsehair wig. She is my ancestor; I worship her. She is my progeny; I bear her.

My mother and I drank from each other's hearts; neither had enough to set life free. Now, as crazed as the gods, we stand side by side, dip our muzzles into a pool of blood, and suck like cattle.

Gramma

I

Gramma crosses the hotel lobby,
past green-velvet divans, huge red roses
swelling up from the carpet's dark background.
Mother pretends she doesn't know her.
Like a tugboat, Gramma,
propelled by the spunky, rhythmic farts
she is so sure nobody can hear.

II

Brother accuses Gramma of stealing
the illicit naked-lady cards he'd gotten himself
down a dark Chinatown alley.
While Gram wails her innocence like a siren,
Mother empties out her suitcase across the floor.
We all look a long time at the profusion
of breasts spread out around our feet.

III

Gramma, dressed in simple widow's black,
has asked me to fasten the gaudy rhinestone cuffs
she'd had me buy her for her birthday.
She wants to wear them all on the plane ride home.
Mother at her wit's end: Her own mother
embroiled her innocent girl in the sin of bad taste.

IV

Mother and Gramma, standing back to back.
"What do you want from me?" Mother growls.
She really wants to know now.
Gramma has not heard a sound for thirty years.

She stares out the window, listens deep
for the answer to a question she can't have heard.
That she's long given up on. Gazing out through the fog
she speaks quietly. Not just to us.

"Want?" she asks. "What do I want? I'd like...
I'd like a little kindness, and an orange."

Autumn Ground

Aunt Tot and Aunt Sis went all pink and moist
working over the fat, steaming pots, canning.
I stood on tiptoe to reach the sink,
wash down baskets full of peaches, plums and pears,
tomatoes and green beans that we'd spoon
into wide-mouthed jars to line the back wall
of the storm cellar. Its doors magical,
lying flat against the ground like that
so no wind could blow them away.
The jars we filled turned each fruit lucent—
the applesauce amber, the cherries glinting rose—
as we tightened their lids and held them up,
joyful in our handiwork, and rotated them
in the slant autumn light.

That must have been why, years later in September,
as I watched the plane nose its way onto the TV screen
and plunge into the second tower, over and over,
and I searched my mind for an action to fit disaster,
I remembered glass jars preserving life's tangible goodness,
and I thought, "Stock up."

It came to me just how bad things were
when I found the grocery store deserted at mid-morning
and felt the absence not only of strangers,
but of Tot and Sis, long behind me, and of the flat doors,
opening upward to gather us in.
There was only me now, mind scuttling, unable to choose,
and the clerk looking abandoned at his station.
He added up my cat food, trail mix, and water.
We assured each other we were OK,
as if touching on what we couldn't grasp would help us.

Then a tall, lean blonde appeared in line behind me.
The amber pendant resting between her clavicles
filled my mind with applesauce in rows,
and I began to breathe back into myself.
She told us she was not OK, that last night
her husband had left her for her favorite sister.
She wondered how to tell her boys that from now on
Dad would be living at their aunt's house.

Her private disaster shimmered inside our public one.
Here was pain we could understand.
The clerk came around the counter and we held one another,
all three swaying together, finding ground.

Grendel-Maaaa

I feared you'd go down the last of our kind,
my Grendel-bairn, my lief. But now, of a sudden,
our fell fate is couth. It's I will fade into the mould,
life-weary, last of the large grunters,
the voracious fur-favored rompers.
It's you will die the only of your kind.

My ledes roared in a world we deemed
was made for us: Joy-of-Heaven shone for us—
hue-drunken flowers,
grasses that made visible the wind,
even the lesser warm-bloods, there
for our play and our devouring.
We lorded it all as it listed us,
all ours to lord.

Then they came a-sheen, the naked, ten-fingered,
from over the bowl-of-the-main.
Wee creatures they were, of derring-do,
but our ablesse—to scatter, to swallow them down.

Yet they bore on their breath some eldritch force.
Invisible. We were stricken from inside!
Our food came back up our maws,
our hair fell out, our muscles withered.
Our starkest fed the fold with their blood.

Some few survived, I among them.
We won the deep caves to dree our woe
we could not wot. Here I bore you,
hight you my Grendel, as the last feres died off,

leaving us two to our separate wyrds.
There was nought in my breast-hoard
to boot you wot this loath life.

I fell into my own wanhope, growling and groping.
Trying to grok you, I beat my brow
'gainst the weedy walls of our water cave.
You pull at me and flee from me, vainglorious boy-ogre,
yammering to yourself with unwinding noise
from the word-hoard of the naked ones.
Soundings echo across our lair.
Twisting and stretching in my ears,
they push me from you sure as
your own paws cast me away.

Today I let you leave the stead without struggle.
In grame I watched you go.
The carls see in you only a troll.
Eftsoons they will pierce you
with their flashers-in-the-fray.
Somewhere you call out one more time:
"Mama, I'm dying!" I have no words for answering.
My dumbness betrays you. You, the only one of your kind.

My tongue flails, helpless in my mouth.
Ack...ack...ack...ack... my Grendel-bairn,
Beloved stranger, my fey one!

How It Happens

Heartbeat to heartbeat, she curls the infant
into her wide chest, becoming part of
his last frail breath. That spaciousness beneath her breastbone
coils in a dense exhale, tugging her groundward.
But the big silverback, lead gorilla, rises to part
the curtains of foliage, and the troop heads off behind.
She curls the small, known hand in her long fingers
and trails after her pack. At dusk she grooms him, tries
to tempt him back with soft shoots of undergrowth.

The young approach, hesitant and curious,
prod at him until mature females wave them off, encircle her.
Masticating. Grooming. Attentive and nonchalant.
He grows harder and lighter. She cradles him,
fingers his stiff features. Beds down with him,
perplexed, among the others.

Come morning, she takes his hand in hers once more.
He has been part of her and he remains so.
She draws him along behind her over fallen tree trunks.
Lays him alongside her when she stops to scratch or chew.
Becomes used to his stillness, his empty gaze.
Notices colors and distances, the motion around her.
The space in her chest lightens as his bones lighten.
He is more like a stump now, a downed limb drying.

Unmarked, the moment she rises alone,
one palm tingling with a nascent emptiness,
and reaches both arms out toward a new shape
just beyond her grasp: a knotty viridescent bough.

Lost

For my sister

She backed off from the Christmas tree, perplexed
by her family after breakfast, how they tore
at the bright paper they'd wrapped with such care
around the packages the night before.
They chirped and fussed. They messed up the living room!
"Stop it!" she hissed, and bent down to collect
the wads of color scattered at her feet.

Her brother looked up from his flannel robe,
that yearly gift he'd come to count on, saw
her snarling mouth, her startled eyes. Recalled
the first year she was old enough to rip
the paper, red and snowflaked, off her gift,
the stuffed bear she named Softly. Over time
she'd slowly rubbed its fur off, and its face
had creased and crumpled, but she'd smiled at it
with the joy of first sight every time.

Now her own face creased and crumpled, like once when they'd
been playing hide-and-seek back in the woods.
He couldn't find her, gave up and went in
through autumn dusk to dinner. Dad gave him
a piece of his mind, and they all went out
to call her home. They found her wedged between
old planks in the barn. Hidden too well.
Too scared to speak or scream out loud. Like he
felt now, seeing her lost in her own mind.
Where her bear would not comfort, where his voice
would not sound. Where she shrank back in this once-
familiar room. Would he ever call his sister home again?

Women of a Certain Age

For Suzanne

We sense the change, an apparent turning,
at the same time as we feel it—a knife
slamming down on the chopping block,
cleaving the known body from itself.
We discern the shift in how the earth holds us,
how we hold ourselves to the earth,
as the fine attention of our passion
revolves, all on its own, toward the roses.
Our tongues relish the details
of a rare bloom's growing habits,
the way they used to curl themselves around
the description of a lover's quirks.

We laugh in gusts, recalling to each other
our grandmothers, great-aunts, those old beloveds
whom we used to imagine belonged to another species,
down on their knees troweling, or bending warily,
their bones evolving into glass,
to harvest those clawed and petalled globes,
those roses they offered up to us.

Women of a certain age
teach each other to circle
within the strict confines of radiance
of afternoon arching backwards into dusk.
Turning, almost imperceptibly,
we hold out to you a light
that warms you less with its heat
than with a layered generosity, reflecting back to you
every angle it has moved through to get here.

THIS POEM IS
NOW THE MAKER

This Poem Is Now the Maker

You come out at me,
shoulders rolling
like the moon growing full.
Arms reach out then,
getting graspy.
Hands force fingers,
thistles drying
into an ominous sky.

Not like the company
I'd asked for, but it's you
who cause me, after all.

Vision for Suzanne's Living Room
(Mandala II)

Come into this family I have traveled far to find,
God, come upon it!
We will sit in a circle around you,
Grown quiet with your weight against our bones.
Together let us see you; let us sit with you, all gathered.
We will press against you, shape you.
We will give you weight and form.

After, we will go our ways at morning.
After, we will go our ways at evening.
After, we will be content to work.
Passing, we will not speak of it;
Touching, we will not tell it;
Glad to feed each other, raise the children, share the work.
Dancing, we will not speak of it;
Bathing, we will not tell it.
Together, we will not jar
The silent circle we have made for you,
The quiet place for you to come in,
The yellow-light core of our heart.

Hands of God

God went out into his dawn shed and puttered.
Hankering. He'd be good with his hands, he mused,
if only he had hands. Out of his longing
came proto snakes with ribs like needles.
Waving themselves along from strings of calcified
knots threaded up their centers.

With the advent of vertebrae, the creatures fanned out.
There were curious fish who dragged themselves
up out of the water, and splashed right back in.
But bones proliferated in the mind of God:
shin bones, thigh bones, sternums and skulls.
And hardened accessories,
hooves and claws, tusks and beaks. The long necks
and massive jaws of dinosaurs.
He took a deep breath into his unembodied self,
exhaled a meteor.

Serpent Clan

For my mother

She brought the iridescent
serpents of sorrow to my cradle
when she could not hold me
in the pain that was feeding
down where her thoughts brewed.
She was not unwise.

Serpents are weavers.
They insinuate themselves
into the void around each other
with grace and with guile.
Their fluid movements
held me, warp and woof.

Because I bore no human scent,
I did not raise their ire or appetite.
To them I was a comfort. A newly mossed stone.
a blink limb twining among them, less lonely
in their company than in the company
of those humans I try so hard to imitate.

Snake Dreams

See how the snake dreams come, offering death.
See how the coils engulf me!
I grow sluggish, encircled by auras of death.
See how the snake eyes haunt me.

Snake, he knows the way back to the mother,
To lie in her stony arms.
Snake, he knows the ways branched out beyond here
When our trails have faded and strayed.
With his slither of skin and his harsh-gentle kiss,
Snake, he is traveling with me.
And I have made a promise to myself:
I will not fall into his pinpoint eyes.

Before the leaves say it,
That the roots may hear, that the snails may hear:
Out in the grass I speak it,
That the cat might know, that the small birds know:
Among the trees I say it,
That the wind might hear, that the moonlight hear:
I will not fall into his pinpoint eyes.

And when it grows too strenuous,
When I cannot breathe for coiling,
And my legs are wrapped in death-snake,
Desire to fall,
I go to the leaves to hear it
In the root song, in the snail song:
In the grasses I remember
What the small birds, the cat eyes know.

I hear it in the treetops
That rage with wind and moonlight:

That the living shall not pass willingly
Back through his pinpoint eyes.

The Shade Garden

*Beauty: the qualities of a person or thing that give
pleasure to the senses.*

The scrunch of wet grass beneath naked bare feet.
The scent of air pregnant with gathering rain.
The dusk cries of children echoing goodnight.
The salt in the sweat on your lover's collarbone.
The blurred stride of the cheetah across your screen.

A thing of beauty is composed of qualities,
a sensual configuration that reaches inward,
digs its roots into the experiencer, that sphere
of knowing we can't quite name.

By the River

dark snakes on dark water swim in synchrony,
you mistake them for a pattern
laid down by the wind.

you pride yourself on noting
nature's brief inscription,
precise yet sensual,

and imagine yourself sliding
free from your clothes   gooseflesh

crawls across your ribcage as you
part the waters with your breastbone,

disturbing what you see as
those liquid notations
rippling out just beyond your grasp:

dark snakes on dark water.
you are spellbound by the time they raise
flat heads to signify themselves,

you who are standing on dry ground.
your life depends
on recognizing the scream you hear as your own.

Prosody

my eyes   my nose   rise up over
                 the rim of the rain barrel

water body   wet within
                 rain's larger wetness

senses on its brimming tongue
                 a quickening

liquid curling hard against
                 swollen wooden staves

sinews flashing   dark green
                 scales parallel stripes

body flickering
                 startle of snake

you wind from side to side
                 calming and troubling the waters

dip your head and circle around
                 your own straight lines

Everything Has a Name

Not just animals, but the legs of settees: cabriole.
Corbeled: the ancient
bone chambers under the hill.

I wanted it all simple:
the bed and the table and the chair
in van Gogh's room.

But there's a name for every variation.
It's my fear
never to forget a name I hear.

Home Alone

Not me in naked-kitchen-dance-with-buzzard
but up by myself late last night squeaking
and stomping and hammering my thighs
bouncing in and back out of my TV chair
within a web of Old Bluesmen and Women
caught up on video and in love with each other
at their Radio City Music Hall reunion. We were
pointing and growling and sawing and howling.
I was pitching high notes out of a lair down in my belly
where I know myself to be Alive. Undaunted.
Before and Beyond any Birth Ever of Alone.

New Year's Meditation

As we leave the *zendo*, newly pruned pigmy plants
in the rock garden shimmer their limbs out for our attention
like children showing off holiday costumes.
Low creepers, high climbers.
Manzanitas open up and outward,
as small as my hand.

Some plants, I know their families,
but I can't call up their names.
Some, still strangers, stretch,
motionless, to be noticed.

My new-washed eyes seem to deepen
to receive them as leaf and stem,
lean into space, brace against the silence
and play it as if it were a bell.

Strange Dreaming

Big cats dream jagged pauses mid-leap
like an old film flapping.
Claw-stretching panic, skating on air
until magnetized back on to instinct's curve,
still vital enough to recall them
in the calls of orangutans, stutters
like a scratch on a record. They haven't ever heard
a record catch, but it enters their innermost
dream ears, years
after vinyl reigned in some far country.

Turning to Myself

Abundance...I should offer it...I don't.
Silence expands me
like the air moving into my lungs.

The gate I have in mind to open
not the simple wooden structure at the base of the hill,
but its perfect rival reflecting in the water.

Into Her Own

What does she own? Her hands,
skin sliding across her knuckles like worn cloth,
wrinkled and spotted. The surfaces they've touched.
The afterimage of their smoother, tapered sisters.
The ache in her hips as she bends to cut off at the roots
the reeds that have invaded her garden.
Her easy way of cooking from scratch.
That mixture of rashness and reticence
somebody once called classy. The memory
of his moustache grazing, prickling her upper lip.
Her covertly ordered messiness when she lives alone.
Eyeglasses and her constant fear of losing them.
Friendships, smooth and various
as desert rocks that once lived on an ocean floor.

What owns her? Place.
The sky, infused with blue and bowing
across tawny foothills. Watershed.
Where ten acres of grass feeds one cow.
Volcanic rock working its way on up
through shallow, dusty soil. Home
to blue-belly and alligator lizards, skinks,
king snakes, Pacific rattlers,
mule deer, shadow of cougar.

Standing Figures, the Tate Modern, 2002

The statues face us, human scale, erect.
They face us solitary, equidistant from one another,
formal on a hammered metal carpet
just past the entrance hall
where their subjects mill and throb,
jamming toward this stern, attending order.

I approach them warily, permutations
on the theme of being human.
They are vital, gesture stirring
at the seat of their stillness,
now and now and here again now.
Their silence, speech. Their fixity, fluid.
We alone in the massive public space.

Each stance strikes in me a resonance,
the kicking forth of a cry.
They instruct me, from my inner organs outward,
in the lost, innate knowledge of what I am.

So I hold out my living face
to the penetration of blind eyes,
silent avowals of marble, plaster, complex alloys.
I meet and am changed by the curve of a chin,
the bend of an elbow, the bare patch where a mouth should be
articulates its own absence. My spine rises.
I give myself back to the earth.

Waking Up

It's come to me late, and for selfish reasons,
to love the dark parts. The parts that can't help but maul
and abandon you. To cultivate affection for the dark parts.
Even your own...especially your own...

lest you live in chronic terror of abandonment
so that the dark abandoner in you
will breathe in your mistrust, your aversion,
your denial of its necessary beauty.
Pulled down by the weight of its own cracking heart,
it will creep backward into the blackness
of inner earth, deep space
where you can never find it.

And you will live alone, unrecognizable
to whatever wants to love you,
to your own baffled heart.

Pearls of What Price

Grubby little nodules, hardening in on themselves,
is what we're left with. They dig like burrs
into the folds of guts and brain.
We carry them unwittingly, these hapless diamonds
composed of what's really happened,
out of what penetrates us. Of what we need to know.
In order to love each other.
In order to save this world.

You know what I mean: this humanness
hiding in our eyes, our mouths, our hands.
Whatever penetrates us. Whatever's seen.
And felt. And told. And heard. Mana.
You know what I mean. Tell me.

Two-Toned Frogs

fear is a gully of two-toned frogs
slick and luminous
is a rope in the night chewed by rodents
a rope you might climb up into numbing daylight
you reach for the rope
it hangs there
by one rotting strand

fear is your wrist jerking back
your face twisting away
as you notice how high you stand
on an old wooden ladder that straddles
realms of abandoned inner space

call up your own weird angels
to stroke your throat
hold your head while you croak out sounds
you've never heard before

hear out your unsuspected songs of gratitude
for up and for down for light and for darkness
for your own absurd certitude that
out beyond beyond
our overwrought creator turns an ear

Home Ground

I've ambled out beyond big barn
at many ages times of year and day
round the head of the little fishing lake
down the rocky slope
all angles.
picking my way
oak trees   bay trees   chaparral
antlers   scattered cow bones

volcanic boulders come to rest
at the foot of the hill
as if just yesterday
gathered in articulated silence
that centers the world

I've clambered across the rocky stream bed
in wild icy winter
dry-mossed barren summer

small pristine valley
in a tough surround

this morning late May
one more birthday
I'm splayed across a flat wide boulder
sucking in sun
vault of my ribcage
rising falling
beneath an opening sky

dawn sun turning
rock face pink
dragonflies wing out across
all hours and all ages

here again among ourselves
we spread out for each other
in the elusive bowl of forever
and the silence rings

Evolution at Seventy

Stubby dragonfly
red-orange buzzes hot pink weeds
widens these old eyes

Would-Be Poem, Groping

She hasn't said yes
or no
neither stop
nor go

Hears herself humming under
a breath she hadn't
known she had

Sound waves push up into song
rhythm shoves her into time
breaking out in rhyme
as if by accident

Tumbles through into conception

In the Presence of the Elements

My language takes the simplest words and sucks on them:
Fruit. Stones.
The salts of the sea.
The ocean, singing:
Marry me.

I listen inward for rhythms, soundings.
Silence...silence...deeper silence...Ahh...
young voice calling out to me. Lost song.

The girl I once was did not write that song;
off the edge of some etheric storm, it caught her ear.
Earth's oversoul awakened, drew the whistling down
into a range that humans almost hear.
She emptied herself to listen,
and song entered her. Overwhelmed her.
She turned away. She married a tone-deaf boy.

Today it sounds inside of me:
the fruit, the stones, the salts of the sea.
The ocean is asking. A lost self nudging.
This time I say *yes*.

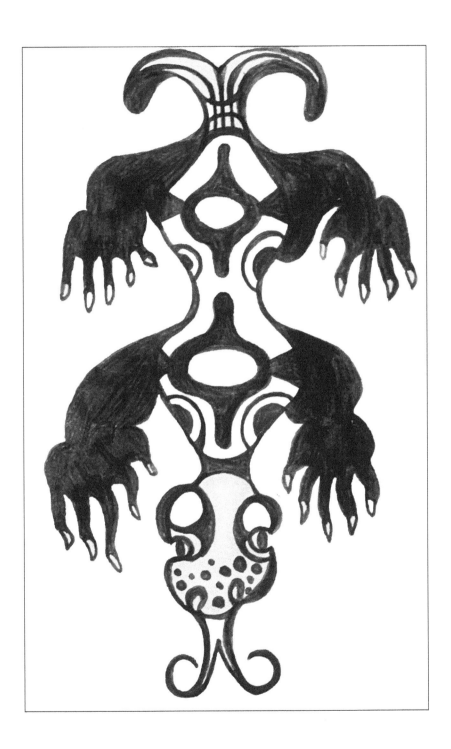

Afterword

My lifelong friend, Maggie Tuteur, began life as Mary Holman Tuteur, an adopted child. Her birth mother gave her up to an urbane Jewish couple from Cleveland, John and Marion Tuteur, who filled her life with high culture and sophistication. Her adoptive mother, a stage actress of some repute, adored her and read to her endlessly, regaling her with tales of tragedy, heroism, and the incongruous nature of life. Fostering a love of language and narrative, she watered the seeds of Maggie's creativity.

Maggie's childhood was filled with magic. When she was six, the Tuteurs moved to a big house on Sea Cliff Avenue, on the edge of the San Francisco Bay. She attended a small private school, where I met her. When I realized she only had two crayons to her name, black and blue, I knew instantly that she would be my friend forever. Not only did I share my crayons, I shared my heart. Sometime that year, Maggie got braces, and we wrote, produced, and performed a play, *Mary Goes to the Dentist*. Her mother was our greatest champion and declared us brilliant.

In the summer of that year, Maggie's parents whisked her off to Europe, where she attended the theater and hung out with actors. She sent me a postcard, which I still have, telling of her adventures and how she "almost" met Montgomery Clift, but he was sick. The experience of her trip to a Europe recovering from the Second World War filled Maggie with memories of her gallant father and the concierges and doormen and colossal staircases she encountered. Later, they would surface in her poem "The Needle's Eye."

The Sea Cliff house was elegant, filled with antiques purchased on various European trips. Marion, a woman of great taste, chose the colors celadon and gray for the interior, which made me feel as if we were wrapped in a cloud. Maggie wasn't particularly fond of the antiques and was forever being scolded for forgetting to use a coaster.

Marion passed the days sitting by the picture window that over-looked the Golden Gate Bridge, working on her needlepoint. Dinner was a formal affair, served promptly at six by Mitzi, the maid, cook, and Maggie's second mother. Maggie adored Mitzi. When her parents traveled, she visited with Mitzi in her room off the kitchen, mining her for stories of her life and her family. Years later, when Mitzi was no longer working for the Tuteurs, Maggie found her in a residence hotel south of Market Street in San Francisco. Maggie insisted her father make all the Social Security payments that he'd not paid over the years so that Mitzi could receive a check every month.

Maggie was faithful to Mitzi till the end. She came to visit one day and found that Mitzi had taken an overdose of her medication. Although conflicted, knowing Mitzi wanted to die, Maggie rushed her to the hospital, where Mitzi later died.

The Tuteurs bought a ranch in Napa during that time. There, Maggie and I were free to roam the hills on horseback and wander the trails to our hearts' content. We spent hours in the pool, turning lobster red, only to be slathered with Marion's Eight Hour Cream later in the evening. When an occasional bird sailed into the ranch house's plate glass window, breaking its neck, we wrapped ourselves in Indian bedspreads and held solemn burials in Marion's garden.

Maggie was happiest at the ranch. We had a clubhouse under the deck of the house where we collected rattlesnake tails and inter-esting rocks. Marion gave us a special shelf in the bathroom for our treasures. We labeled it "In God We Turst." Neither of us were stellar spellers, but we truly felt close to some divine source in those days.

The ranch foreman, Julius, and his wife, Margaret, were pivotal to Maggie's love of the natural world. They taught us their country ways. Julius taught us how to be with the horses. When we were around ten years old, he took us to witness the breeding of Maggie's mare, Moonlight. We sat in the rafters of the barn with some annoy-ing boys to witness the rather violent spectacle. We learned the facts of life that day.

Every Saturday night, we'd head for the Uptown Theater in downtown Napa to see the latest shows. The Tuteurs loved all movies, and Maggie did, too. We faithfully read the best movie magazines and filled up on the gossip. Over the years, Maggie grew to be a huge Tennessee Williams fan. She particularly identified with *The Fugitive Kind*, a Marlon Brando and Anna Magnani film about a drifter. Maggie was always a fan of outsiders. Many of her poems pay tribute to them. But it was Maggie the Cat, in *Cat on a Hot Tin Roof*, who truly captivated her. As an adult, she changed her name from Mary to Maggie. To her, the name represented the beauty, sexiness, and depth of spirit she identified with.

The fact that she was adopted occupied Maggie's thoughts for many years. She was a blue-eyed blonde with a round shape, while her family was dark-haired, dark-eyed, and lean. Sometimes, thoughts of abandonment crept into her moods and colored her world. It also led to her affinity for outsiders, those who seemed to struggle with life, to march to a different drummer. These folks were always treated with reverence for their stories. And they people her poems.

When we were twelve or thirteen, a sadness fell over the Tuteur house. Marion was beset with serious depressions that shrouded the Sea Cliff house in a somberness that no one spoke of. Maggie was expected to be beautiful, intelligent, and quiet. As she blossomed into puberty, her body became womanly. Marion was delighted with her beautiful daughter, whose blooming sexuality was apparent, but she was also threatened by her. During this time, Maggie became a voracious reader, a sensitive observer, and a collector of impressions that she carefully stowed away.

Maggie had a treasured friend, Francie Chouteau, who lived in the neighborhood and also attended our school. They spent hours at Francie's house, where her mother welcomed "Miss Mary," as she called her, and treated her as one of her own. Maggie thrived with the Chouteaus. Francie's two brothers were definitely a plus. Often, the family would head to the Russian River, where the Chouteaus

had a house. Maggie and Francie spent hours on the river, flirting with boys, sharing adventures, and delighting in their beginnings of womanhood. They also roamed the Tuteur ranch together, galloping their horses across fields and talking endlessly about life.

Maggie chose to go to Chadwick, a boarding school in Los Angeles, when she was a junior. She became a favorite of her English teacher, Mr. Nelson, who raved about her poems and found her to be an astute reader of literature. There, Maggie became a true student. The school inspired her. She made many friends who tended to look just like her, blonde, beautiful, and alive. She fell in love with Gary Jones, who unfortunately was already taken by another girl. But somehow the two of them managed to find time to occasionally be affectionate with one another. Maggie pined for Gary, but he married his high school sweetheart. Years later, that marriage fell apart, and Maggie and Gary renewed a deep friendship, though they never quite resumed their romance.

Sadly, while Maggie was away at school, her mother committed suicide in December 1963. Maggie threw herself into her studies. After a trip to Europe with her father the following summer, she entered Sarah Lawrence College. There, she studied early childhood development and worked in the college nursery school. But the East Coast was not welcoming to Maggie. She spent a good portion of her fall semester in the infirmary with mononucleosis. Although she appreciated her classes, she grew to loathe the boys from the Ivy League colleges whom she was thrown in with. She found them all to be sex-crazed and heartless. After one year, she headed back to California and U.C. Berkeley, taking a deep love of psychology and child development with her.

While she was on the East Coast, Maggie spent a good deal of time with her brother, Michael Kahn, a professor in the psychology department at Yale. Maggie was in awe of Michael and soaked up everything he could teach her. She became good friends with his friends, learning more about psychology and creativity. "The New Haven Group," composed of Michael's fellow professors, graduate students, girlfriends, and wives, met frequently to have dinner and discuss ideas long into the night. They were a band of intellectual free spirits who loved one another. Maggie adored them all, adopting their interests and lifestyles, which she brought back to Berkeley. Once there, she declared herself a hippie and proclaimed her disdain for conventional society and behavior.

Maggie bloomed at Berkeley. Michael had introduced her to Buddhism, LSD, and the Human Potential Movement, all of which profoundly influenced her. She became political, particularly around the issue of civil rights. She also became a poet, attending every poetry reading she could find. She spent time with intellectual students and bedded a few. She eventually settled in a sunny studio on Benvenue, which had a large window overlooking the street. Her blue typewriter sat on the dining table in front of it amid a jumble of papers and sketchbooks. The place was always a shambles, with clothes, books, and magazines everywhere. At one time, she had two ducks that flew freely about the room and shat everywhere.

During the Benvenue years, Maggie became a rock 'n' roll fan, with music blaring from her studio night and day. She had every Dylan album there was and referred to him as "Bobby Dylan," as though they were old pals. She liked the Beatles, too. We'd get stoned and sit on the floor listening to *Sergeant Pepper*, memorizing and analyzing the lyrics. She was a fan of the Rolling Stones as well, and she especially liked Mick Jagger, whom she found sexy and gorgeous. That summer, she and a few friends set out for the Stones concert at Altamont but got stuck in the traffic jam. They had to resort to listening to the performances on KSAN, caught in traffic miles from the venue. The events of that day shocked Maggie. She sensed that a great darkness had entered her world, and it distressed her.

Maggie discovered Rapidograph pens at a shop on Telegraph Avenue and began making drawings of faces and bodies and all sorts of creatures that came straight out of her imagination and were most likely inspired by an acid trip or two. Some of her best drawings were made around the edges of the notes she took in class. In later years, she turned to drawing in an attempt to unravel her complex psyche.

At Berkeley, Maggie was not the most disciplined of students. She mostly got A's on her English papers, but she never turned them in on time. Requirements for graduation didn't thrill her but she fulfilled them. She had a few favorite teachers, some of whom expanded her world of poetry. She loved T. S. Eliot and read "The Waste Land" over and over. She pored over Yeats, marveling at his lyricism. But it was while studying under Seamus Heaney, a visiting professor from Ireland and future Nobel laureate, that Maggie found her voice. He encouraged her, teaching her how to write about place with reverence and to reveal intangible truth with imagery.

After Maggie graduated from Berkeley, she spent a year at Stanford, working toward an MA in English. Her focus was T. S. Eliot. *Four Quartets* and "The Waste Land" captivated her. That summer, in

1972, Maggie and I took a trip to England, Scotland, and Ireland, where I could tread in the footsteps of Keats, on whom I'd written my senior thesis, and Maggie could submerge herself in all things Yeats. Her father created our itinerary, booking us into the most luxurious and famous old hotels. We attended every possible poetry reading, bought many books, visited castles and cathedrals, and ended each day reading our books at the dinner table. We photographed one another among the stones at Stonehenge and visited a ruin that once belonged to my Herrick ancestors. One night in Wales, we danced in the Portmerion moonlight, singing at the top of our lungs. In Dublin, we met Seamus Heaney at his club for a drink, which left Maggie breathless and giddy.

It was on that trip that Maggie became reacquainted with Robert Domergue, a dancing-school friend from San Francisco, who would eventually become her husband. He was living in Paris on the Île de la Cité, working as an artist and avoiding the draft. When Robert returned to the States, he courted Maggie, who was then at Stanford.

She soon abandoned the MA program and moved to San Francisco to live with him. They eventually married in 1982. Robert was handsome and urbane, having descended from influential French and Mexican families. He had fabulous taste and social connections, and after a year, he opened an antiques shop in Jackson Square.

The marriage was a stormy one, with numerous rows. One thing the couple shared was a love of fine dining. Maggie and Robert slaved over complex Northern Italian recipes in their cramped Sacramento Street apartment and entertained a lot. Beyond their bedroom window was a rooftop where Robert built a greenhouse, and Maggie filled it with cacti. Whenever a cactus flower appeared, she was entranced. She loved cacti, the spinier and lumpier the better. She loved them because they were different and not soft and lovely like most flowers. Their prickliness appealed to her.

Robert was a member of the San Francisco Waltz Society. He delighted in dressing Maggie in elegant gowns and bedecking her with her mother's rubies and diamonds for an evening of dancing. High society was not really Maggie's cup of tea, but Robert adored hobnobbing with the A-list folks.

Maggie and Robert spent a lot of time at the ranch, where they moved into Julius and Margaret's old farmhouse. A carpenter friend of Robert's made a writing studio for Maggie there. It was a wonderful pale peach room with a long desk along one wall. A bookcase that held hundreds of books covered another wall from floor to ceiling. Maggie chose to have the windows installed at desk level so that she could look out over the green hills of the ranch as she wrote. Many of her poems were written in that room.

Sometime during this period, Francie Chouteau, our dear friend, overdosed on her grandmother's sleeping pills. She left two sons behind, one of whom found her. All her friends and family were heartsick, but Maggie was overcome with sorrow. We talked endlessly about Francie, remembering how beautiful she was and all the fun the three of us had had. We couldn't help but feel at fault that we'd not been there for her. Maggie wrote dozens of poems to and about Francie. She carried that loss her entire life.

Once back in San Francisco and living with Robert, Maggie went looking for a job. Her father owned a flag factory in the city and put her to work in the dye department. There Maggie became close to the head dyer, Bennie, and her son, Alan. She was drawn to Alan because he'd had a brush with the law and was an outsider. After a couple of years working there, it became clear that the chemicals in the dyes were making Maggie sick. Though she didn't know it, she had developed chronic fatigue syndrome, which was to trouble her the rest of her life. She began a program at San Francisco State, where she received her Marriage and Family Counseling Certificate. Around this time, her marriage to Robert unraveled and the couple divorced.

Maggie first practiced psychotherapy at the Marin Family Counseling Center as an intern. She saw a few clients there, both adults and children. After completing her internship, she practiced on her own at her house and occasionally saw clients at their homes. She became interested in Sand Tray Therapy and studied with world leaders in the field. She acquired an impressive collection of miniature toys and figures for the therapy, which she thoroughly enjoyed. Through sand-tray play, she gained great insights into her clients. Maggie was an effective therapist, but the work took its toll on her. She found it difficult to detach from the suffering of her patients.

Maggie lived in San Anselmo while she was a practicing therapist. Once there, she began to fervently write poetry again. She was prolific, spending hours perched over her computer with a thesaurus on her lap. She studied weekly with Kim Addonizio and attended any lecture or poetry reading that came her way. She took classes and workshops with Jane Hirshfield and other poets through UC Extension. Two other outlets helped her to expand her self-knowledge: Authentic Movement, a dance-therapy practice, and the Esalen Institute, where she attended workshops for many years, becoming friends with a new tribe of people.

When she was in her forties, Maggie's half-brothers, Randy and Richie Green, discovered that she existed. As she writes in her poem "Negative Space," she had found her birth mother eighteen years before and written to her, asking to meet her. Her mother refused to meet her, but she did keep the letter. It was found by Maggie's half-brothers in the trailer where their mother had raised them. Their mother, Margaret, had developed Alzheimer's and was in a nursing home. Maggie was ecstatic to make contact with her brothers. Both Randy and Richie came to California, and she went to Atlanta where she was welcomed into the family. Maggie was able to visit her mother before she died. Although Margaret could no longer speak, she seemed to show a flicker of recognition. Maggie held her hand and gazed into a face that looked like her own. At last she had found her birth family, and they looked like her.

At one point, Randy accompanied Maggie to Ohio, where she met her aunts. They, too, welcomed her and told her about her birth. Her mother had been a nurse in Hawaii, where she had an affair with an officer. After the war, she returned to Ohio, alone and pregnant.

After Maggie's birth, her mother briefly brought her home and gave her the name Francis. Maggie loved knowing that, because of Francie.

The door to Maggie's house in San Anselmo was always open to visitors. She planted a garden and had a cat, Tender Buttons. Many friends came by for potluck meals and conversation, and Maggie shared her poems with them. She had a soft spot for troubled down-and-out folks, respecting their journeys. She saw their humanity as heroic and wrote poems about them. She had a healthy relationship to sex and took many lovers, though one at a time. They seemed to drift in and out of her life, and she told me about all of them with relish. Her stories delighted me, as I could vicariously experience activities that I was too cowardly to engage in on my own.

Maggie was interested in psychotropic drugs. In the mid-seventies, Maggie, Francie, and I dropped acid together in Berkeley at the Benvenue studio. We then attempted to go out for dinner, but Maggie and I dissolved into gales of laughter. Francie deftly took charge, paid the waiter, and guided us, laughing and staggering, home. We found the ranch a perfect place to indulge and would take long magical walks to special spots that we treasured. Over the years, Maggie experimented with San Pedro cactus, mushrooms, and peyote with a variety of friends and gleaned insight from each experience.

After leaving San Anselmo, Maggie moved many times, eventually settling in Sebastopol, where she finally felt at home. Along the way, her life and possessions were pared down, but now, with her favorite treasures around her, she is able to live among everything she loves, everything that brings meaning to her days, and I am thankful for that.

Over the years, Maggie has struggled with her health. She was diagnosed with many diseases, all of them difficult to identify and treat: chronic fatigue, Hashimoto's disease, and Lyme disease were just a few. She saw numerous physicians and alternative healers, all of whom prescribed drugs, herbs, teas, and diets. Pill upon pill was

added to her regime and none were ever deleted. She struggled with depression, threatening suicide periodically. Her adoption plagued her for years. She felt abandoned by her birth mother, which led to years and years of therapy with a number of therapists. A deep loneliness and terror filled her with bleak thoughts and kept her up at night. She often felt fatigued. When she felt good, she'd overdo and be back in bed for days. She slowly lost her ability to hear, which isolated her. As the years passed, Maggie began to lose her memory. It began with a lost word or two and ended with entire blocks of time.

Maggie may be the most complicated and maddening person I have ever known. She believed fervently in psychology, specifically therapy, and spent her life figuring herself out. She was able to tap into a place within that was fantasy and truth at the same time. She was always one to embellish the truth, but that came from her urge to create a good story, which her poems never fail to do. She could be stubborn and fly off at the drop of a hat, but she was also unbelievably kind. At times she was shy and a pleaser. At times she imagined herself a vamp. She valued smart people and considered nonconformists, people who had challenging lives, or were good talkers, "smart." She found tragedy to be an asset and believed that people who have a sense of the tragedy of life were always "smart." She could be wily and prickly, but she could tell stories to entrance every listener.

Maggie and I have shared a lifetime of play and adventure. I have been a witness to her brilliance and her debilitating depression. I have infuriated her when I tried to offer advice and delighted her when I praised her creativity. I have photographed her in nearly every stage of our life together, knowing in my heart that these images are a testament to our great love for one another. They reveal an extraordinary lifelong friendship.

—Louise Kleinsorge Williams
    February 2023

About the Author

I began making poems when I was learning, awkwardly, how to make words. I wanted to say how the sunlight in the kitchen garden bounced off the grass blades and made them shine.

That impulse led to poetry submersion in Berkeley in the '60s and an MA from Stanford in Creative Writing in 1978. Then I forgot about the whole thing and became a psychotherapist. A friend challenged (or bullied) me back into writing when he noticed that I thought like a poet. So I plunged back into poetry in the '90s.

Favorite teachers have been Seamus Heaney, Jean Valentine, Jane Hirshfield, Kim Addonizio, and Terry Ehret. My poems have appeared in various publications, including *The Dark Horse, The Hudson Review, The Nation*, the anthology *WomanPrayers*, Marin Poetry Center anthologies, and *Zero-Earth Journal*.

—Maggie Tuteur
  January 2021

Acknowledgments

The following poems first appeared in these publications, sometimes in different versions:

The Hudson Review: "Knowing What We Know," "Settling Up," and "Women of a Certain Age"

Marin Poetry Center Anthology: "After Your Stroke," "Claiming Kin," "Girls Springing," "Ice Ages," "Invocation," "Naked Ladies," "The Needle's Eye," "New Year's, 2007," "One Flesh," and "Shades of Childhood"

The Nation: "Grace for My Twenty-Fifth Year"

Rediscovering Beowulf: The Poetry and Mystery of an Ancient Tale: "Grendel-Maaaa"

WomanPrayers: "Source" and "First Passion"

"Grace for My Twenty-Fifth Year" was reprinted in *WomanPrayers.*

"Women of a Certain Age" was reprinted in the *Marin Poetry Center Anthology.*

I am indebted to John Tuteur, Bruce Gibbs, and Angel Booth for their creative guidance and support in compiling my poems for publication, with special thanks to Bruce for his heartfelt foreword. Thanks also to Jean Clifford for liberating the texts from their software sarcophagus; to Louise Kleinsorge Williams for her photographs, artistic vision, and illuminating afterword; to Terry Ehret, Jo-Anne Rosen, Carolyn Miller, and Steve Gilmartin for their editing, design, and proofreading skills; and to the teachers, family, and friends who have inspired and supported my poetic adventures over the years.

Alphabetical Index of Poems

For more information on ordering
additional copies of this book,
please visit wordrunner.com.

Printed in the USA
CPSIA information can be obtained
at www.ICGtesting.com
CBHW041235081123
1668CB00004BA/8